OUT OF NOWHERE

OUT OF NOWHERE

NEW AND SELECTED POEMS

Mary Ann Taylor-Hall

OLD COVE PRESS

LEXINGTON, KENTUCKY

Old Cove Press
Lexington, Kentucky
oldcove.com

ISBN: 978-0-9675424-6-1

Cover photograph:
Cave Horse, James Baker Hall, c. 1990s

Photograph of Mary Ann Taylor-Hall:
Dan Silvestri at Impact Photography, 2017

Design: Nyoka Hawkins

Special thanks
to Stephanie Adams and Sharon Hatfield
for editorial assistance

The following pages end with a stanza break:
17, 28, 32, 34, 53, 55, 66, 68, 74, 77, 83, 85, 90, 94, 96, 101,
105, 114, 118, 122, 132, 134, 136, 141, 148, 150, 165, 170, 172, 176

Publisher's Cataloging-in-Publication data
Names: Taylor-Hall, Mary Ann, author.
Title: Out of nowhere : new and selected poems / Mary Ann Taylor-Hall.
Description: Lexington, KY: Old Cove Press, 2017.
Identifiers: ISBN 978-0-9675424-6-1
Subjects: LCSH American poetry--21st century. | American poetry--
Women authors. | American poetry. | Poetry, American.
| BISAC POETRY / American / General
Classification: LCC PS3570.A983 O98 2017 |
DDC 813.54--dc23

FIRST EDITION

for Jim

Grateful acknowledgment to Larkspur Press for *Dividing Ridge* (2008) and to the Press on Scroll Road for *Joy Dogs* (2013), in which the following poems first appeared:

From *Dividing Ridge*

· Waking
  (retitled The Tethered Gamecocks)
· These Rare Things Happening
· Bowls
· Indigo Bunting
· The Barking Dogs
· Ruin Is Not the End of Anything
· Botticelli's *Venus*
· Acting Class
· What Happened After That?
· Brooklyn Heat
  (retitled Brooklyn, Broken)
· Let's Try Again
· How It Comes On
· Ceaseless Rain
  (retitled Here, With You)
· Land Chanty
· Now Secret Bell
  (retitled Bell of Breath)
· Blind Stitch
· Sublet
· Valentine's Day
· Like Tall Grass Bending
· A Flask of This
· The Rain Goes On Without You

From *Joy Dogs*

· Tightrope
· Conversation
· Still Here
· Now You Are Leaves
· Down There
· Joy Dogs
· When I Was Here
· Falling Back
· Separation
· Fallow
· Second Winter
· Island
· Sweet Juicy Life
· Little Leasts
· Landing
· Waking, Sleeping
  (retitled Past Perfect)
· Birthday Greetings

Contents

Part One: Nothing but Alive

Part Two: The Lover from Train Windows

Part Five: Joy Dogs

Part Six: Whatever Calls

Part Seven: The Known Path, The Way Home

Part Eight: The Rain Goes On Without You

Part One: Nothing but Alive

TO THE MUSE

Come to me
my other my orphan
my one and only
spirit cloud
my own angel
come through
this fort of bone
this crush of person
come through find form
live here
be alive
with me

What comes then
is a black Lab
head on my thigh
drooling creek water
wanting wanting
finally he goes
to lie in his spot
by the stove
smelling of distant skunk
licking his privates
oh well oh well

OUT OF NOWHERE

I open my eyes to a lunar glare. I rise and feel my way through the moonlit rooms. Out beyond the glass door, on the plain of bright snow, bare branches of the elms press down their long, definite, forking shadows.

And through them I glimpse a half-opaque, half-translucent procession of creatures, moving one by one across the wide clearing—hunched, hurrying, low to the ground, or gliding, leaping, stretching upward along the stone wall. The size of—oh, porpoises, maybe.

I watch, stunned for a moment. Then my mind takes over, the one that wants me to go outside, find out what it is I'm really seeing. Here, in the real world.

I pull on my jacket and boots, step out onto the stones, look up toward the bright moon, almost full, falling now behind the chimney at the roof's peak, casting onto the backyard—ah—shadows of smoke! Shadows of smoke, blown southward in irregular gusts. Gusts. Not ghosts.

As I stand watching, hugging myself against the cold, out of nowhere a thin gray hound breaks from the woods and streaks across the clearing in the opposite direction, right through the shadowy parade, so low and fast and silent I think at first it's another shadow.

It disappears into the woods on the north side, headed,
I guess, for the open field beyond. From inside the
house, my own dogs catch the scent now. Frantic, they
bark and scrabble at the door. *Too late, buddies,* I tell
them. But I let them out and they race by me, eager for
the chase, noses to the ground, tails high.

I turn and walk the other way, down the gravel track
into the strangeness at the edge of the circling world,
where the great burr oak lifts its long bare limbs
towards the heavens, saying something I nearly
understand. It looks like *hallelujah,* but it isn't.
A planted stillness within the moving air. A quiet,
stern declaration: *I am oak.* Or maybe just *I am.*

The heavens, we say—heaven upon heaven, space
opening upon space, doorway beyond doorway.
My dogs somewhere out there follow the scent of the
thing they'll never catch.

Then, off at a distance, low on the snow-covered hill
across the road, a sudden flare of golden light traces
something like a small Chinese ideogram on the
darkness and disappears. A breath or two later, another.

After that, nothing. The whole night is waiting. There
is, no doubt, an explanation for this phenomenon as
well. Can anyone tell me what it is?

5

And where has the hound gone? And where are my dogs?

The earth settles back to what I know of it. The moon moves now a little further across the open sky toward the western horizon beyond the barn. I stay where I am a while longer, my breath sending its own small ghosts into the dark. Then I call my dogs back from wherever they've gotten to.

I hear them panting toward me from a long way off.

NOTHING BUT ALIVE

We are, each one, alone—this is not news,
and neither is it news that sometimes we break free.
Our spirits slide into the clear black sky of stars
and (perhaps obscured by clouds) the moon,
rolling through its phases above our circumstantial bodies,
with their outrageous stories and long bones and birthmarks
and honest, crazy loves and tendencies
toward every sort of breakdown.

We see it all from up there, for a moment, everything
that holds us to our lives with a force like gravity.
And we're, for a moment, not held. Floating free.
Nothing but alive.

     But we've come to love our fragile cloister.
We fear to lose its homey beauty, its eccentric rooms,
its constancy and shelter. We go back down to it.
We settle in.

THESE RARE THINGS HAPPENING

The dark slides off the air, the stiff blue sky
again a cloudless arc. This drought has moved
beyond language. I go for days not hearing
from a living soul. I hear from dead ones though,
their keening words, *I wish, I want,* rustling
like brown leaves still clinging to the branch.
I want to hear rain dripping from trees.
Yesterday a deer broke so near to me
I caught its dusty scent. On the uphill road,
a hawk sailed out of a tree and skidded
past my face.
                          Explanations
are beyond me. This is a serious season here,
quiet and unbroken, and then
these rare things happening.
I think of them as warnings.

This morning, at the compost heap,
a box turtle, strong neck at full extension,
orange eyes watching me,
lay on top of another turtle,
which was overturned, its undershell
bright yellow. The upright turtle
held the other with its ancient claws.
I don't know why.

                The full moon sank
to the left of me just as the sun rose
to the right. The blue sky hardened again
over the earth in its distress. When I returned,
later, to check, the upright turtle had disappeared.

I turned the other right side up.

By noon it too was gone.

FAR FROM IT

The air is stillness, holding,
silent things listening to silence—

the big gray moth spread flat and still,
almost invisible against the weathered board,
the unmoving new leaves of the elm, the frogs
gone back under pond mud.

      Where are the birds now?
Hush. The light is glare and glaze.
Hours, hours,
      holding there—

until time sallies up the hill, sudden, blunt,
like an army. An outward rush of wind—
and the gauzy sky comes loose, separates,
gathers into dense mounds and towers,
revealing something beyond itself,
      a pale, distant blue.

Just then a jet,
      crossing east to west,
          rips the day open.

Yes, it's Tuesday.

We are not finished here. Far from it.

GOD OF THE GALAXIES

And there was light.

Now here we are, only we don't know where we are,
in the midst of all the unimaginable dark out-thereness,
the thick of it, the thin of it, the billions of galaxies,
dark energy, dark matter—all that secretiveness
and explosive mystery.

Nowhere whistles through the air, a galactic wind—
now here our fragile defense against the milky vastness,
the timeless, personless dark.

We caught the light. Wherever we are, here we are.
We came into our speeding moment, our flake of time.

Here we are, we call it earth, the movement, the moment,
the rain coming, passing, gone,
the blue-gray violets, the wild geese honking up off the pond.
And all the bloody, holy rest of it.

ETERNITY

Low fog thickened the long evening light.
Light became almost a substance.
Five deer gathered form before me
then erased themselves again in the shrouded woods.
The dark, smudged line of the last ridge top—*beyond, beyond*—
all that was left of the world of particulars.

       I used to think that the world—
its roads and fences and stoves, its necklaces and buses
and tall buildings—was a scrim that sometimes,
by some unexpected miracle, could be drawn aside.
And for a moment then, we'd glimpse eternity.

       But on this evening, it seemed
the very air I breathed was laden with eternity.
Eternity was what I moved through.

       I turned back.
I climbed the last rise and saw my house,
the windows lit up, glowing faintly through the fog
and falling darkness.

Part Two: The Lover from Train Windows

PASSING OUT

I am a yellow leaf,
sliding slantwise
on a dark, shallow wind.
There is a kind of joy in it,
turning and gliding
through the shredded clouds.

Time is not on my side now.
Time is on the other side.

I settle somewhere, waiting
for the other circling leaves—
or are they stars—
to stop their yellow flashing.
They go out one by one.
The night is cool,
the wind is sweet,
here on the slatted porch floor.
The real stars are silent
and still and white.

I can't measure
the distance I have come
or what I've given up
to be exactly where I am.

THE LOVER FROM TRAIN WINDOWS

Through my reflection in the train window,
I saw three cabins close together in a clearing,
a bonfire blazing in the early morning
inside the drifting fog, as the train sped by.

The place seemed real and urgent, the lives it held
substantial. There, beside the fire,
three women in faded dresses stood talking,
arms folded against the morning chill.

My face was the face of a ghost, sliding by,
transparent. I could see right through me.
The train hurried on to wherever it was
I was headed.
              Always the lover
from train windows, barreling on
to where I didn't know
I didn't wish to go.

CHAMBERS OF THE BRAIN

The brain, I know, is more corridors than chambers,
but I think of mine as a rambling old eccentric boarding house
with water-stained wallpaper, its narrow downstairs hall
lit by an ancient fixture with three of its five bulbs missing,
its walls a jumble of decorative plates picked up at flea markets,
along with souvenirs from Gatlinburg and NYC and prints
of half-clothed maidens calling from the woods,
the closed doors of the boarders' bedrooms
painted the color of dried blood.
                                        But there,
I'm getting carried away.
Still, my brain is a boarding house, it's true.
Things come and stay for a while, then disappear
without paying last week's rent.

I've had some close-up knowledge of other brains—
stainless steel concourses, tubular, modern,
no sharp corners or dead ends, helpful signs, instead,
to tell you how to get to where you're going.
Or brains with calm, uncluttered spaces
where people do yoga so fluid it is almost
out of body, into air. And some are rivers,
gathering and gathering from their tributaries,
running their certain course toward the wide sea.
Some are churches or libraries with vaulted ceilings
and vast, dedicated silence and light streaming in.

17

And some are like ancient maps,
with brave little ships
sailing off to *terra incognita*.

As for me, I guess I'll take my boarding house.
Once past that hallway, I've discovered that the place
is full of arches and crannies, passageways leading to secret dens
with hidden doors, or a narrow winding stairwell to the tower.

I live in lostness. Both my waking life and my dreams
are full of not knowing where I am. It's the price I pay
for living in my historically compelling monument—
I try again and again to get to where I thought I meant to go.
Well, I get to somewhere else. There is no telling
what I find there.

LET'S TRY AGAIN

It's some kind of conference. I have taken under my wing
a child, a little dancer. I hold her thin dark hand
in my lighter one. She wants to stay with me.
I think I can take care of her. I want to try,
because she seems so bright and promising,
and full of need.
                        But then I am alone,
awaiting a lesson in self-defense. A sergeant,
ruddy, tow-headed, enters the room, carrying
a rope. I have to learn a complicated knot
and then perform some tricky, fast footwork
into and out of the big loop I have made.
I'm hopeless. I can't concentrate. I don't know
where the child has gotten to. I want to quit
the lesson and go look for her. But I'm afraid
of the sergeant, and anyway, I feel I need to learn
this demanding art of self-defense.

'Let's try again,' he sighs.

                        I wake in panic,
because the child is lost. I am all gone
to heartbeat now. Lying on my side, I hear
in my right ear my blood shoot through its course.
'Whoops! Whoops!' it says, as if each earnest beat
marked another merry pratfall.

Now the clouds
are loafing in, after two days of heat.
Before the rain, I shovel manure,
hoping it will wash down
around the roots of the foxgloves.
Later, this notebook in my lap, I'm asking
why the little dancer in my dream had to be lost.
Where is she now?
Still leaning against a wall somewhere,
her socks drooped down,
waiting for me to find her?

I hope she knows I'm trying.

INCENSE

The tip catches.
I blow out the flame.
The remaining ember
crawls steadily
down the shaft,
dropping the memory
of itself into
the wooden tray.
The little glow
(the instant
that never knows
it's over)
finally reaches
the base,
where it goes—
quietly—
out.

(But sometimes the ember dies for no reason,
halfway down the stick. Sometimes the flame
just won't catch, or I light it and turn away,
forget to blow it out, so that the stick
becomes a quick candle.)

I woke this morning thinking how many times
my life might have been over. First,
in the Lying-In Hospital in Chicago,
a newborn with dysentery

when there was no medication for it.
You Almost Died We Almost Lost You
was my name then. My life
might not have been lived—
all this life that's now dropped into
the ash-catcher. This ember would not
at this moment be holding
a blue plastic pen, would not
be propped up against pillows,
Mother's begonia waiting for me
to draw the curtain back
and let the new day touch it.

HER BROTHER'S DRUM

Everything is strange now—the curtain blowing,
her own feet waving out there, the forms gathering
to be the world. The brother looking through
the railings of the crib. The brother, beating his drum.
Oh happy now, to be in the world, to come to it as it sharpens
and comes to her, through mouth and belly and eyes.
Through sounds, for she came out of a place where sounds
were liquid, and then a muffled thrum from somewhere else.

The small warm closeness of that other world—
the one she swam in for a while—fled from her suddenly.
Then somewhere else was everywhere,
coldness and clashing sounds,
busy hums and clicks
from the big blurred shapes
and she so small and screaming
and suddenly come loose and all alone.

But now it comes to her. She has a blanket
and her mother's warm body where she holds her close.
She loves the beating of her brother's drum.
She has feet to wave. She waves them.

WHAT HAPPENED AFTER THAT?

Weather blew in today, twilight at four,
leaves skidding across the narrow road,
sudden rain against the skylight
like a motor kicking on,
Whitney's poems at the round table.
'I think,' he says, 'my life
has no validity.' Then the news
with Jim, the leftovers, *Jeopardy*,
the dishes, the sheets in the dryer.

Sleepless, trying to remember
my life, I rehearse again and again
the way my mother taught me to tuck the blanket
around my doll, the head toward one point,
the other points folded in to keep her snug,
a little bundle tightly wrapped.

I put my dolly in her buggy.
I wheeled her down the hall
and out the door. What happened
after that I couldn't say.

THE BOHEMIAN GLASS VASE

Shards of the rosy Bohemian glass, the treasure,
the long-ago ball, thrown by the lost brother,
missed by the lost girl. Their mother sits on the
floor, the pieces of glass in her lap.
'This was all I had of hers,' she explains.
Not to them. To the air—
her lost past looming backwards,
there, in the dim alcove.
Her own lost mother. The girl sits close,
wanting to wind time back
to where the ball the brother threw was—caught!
To where he did not throw the ball at all.
But she is huddled there beside her mother,
who is fingering the shards.

She is in fact still there, that girl,
though she has gone on,
through all these corridors and rooms,
these breakages.

BLIND STITCH

She knelt on the bare floor of our narrow hall,
mouth full of pins, while I turned before her,
slowly, patiently, used by then to standing still,
to turning in place, one step, one step,
both of us in one dream of the new life
hidden in three yards of cloth:

the red plaid taffeta skirt,
the yellow organdy Easter dress,
the polished cotton, lilac,
with strips of ivory set in,
the blue satin gown.

She pinned the hem according to the rule.
I turned when she said turn.
I trusted her to get it right.

Long the thread, tight and hidden the knot.
One stitch, one stitch, one blind stitch
after another, in the lamplight,
the silver pins released from service
as she came to them, her thick hands
moving with small and careful grace,
pricking the pin back into the red cushion,
the hem held now by the ancient
invisible miracle of thread.

ELEVEN

I carry my baby brother on my hip. I'm hoping
someone will think I am his mother.
A life blooms out around me as I walk along the sidewalk
to the lake—*a little house, spaghetti simmering*
on the back burner, a lanky husband in a white T-shirt,
just home from work, smiling, leaning out,
opening the door for me and for this baby
I am now so expertly tending.

Later, my mother hands me a couple of Kraft caramels.
We're watching Dinah Shore. I unwrap one
and put it in my mouth. I move my tongue around it
as it melts. Oh sensuous life! I can have more if I want.

The caramels—in the narrow pantry,
on the shelf above the liquor!
Each little memory is an ecstatic burst.

I'm trying to remember who I was.

EKTACHROME

The light hits, the shutter clicks,
trapping an eyedropper of light,
like a water sample from a moving stream.
The light is caught and fixed.
What the light once hit still says
from its cage of chemicals: *today*.

It is my mother, in her pink plaid shirt.
She stands beside the azaleas.
Her pleasure shows.
In all their glory, she probably is saying.
She straightens her shoulders.
She smiles and holds her breath,
then leaves it behind when she moves out of the lens
into the rest of that time she called *today*.

She raked the leaves.
Toward evening there was rain.
By then she was making soup, maybe.
No one remembers what she did past the smile.
But now, long separated within a plastic sheath
from her real time, she calls out:
Help me. Come back for me.

But she cannot move out of the face she gave to the light
once, fifty years ago. Her smile insists:
today, this second, this fraction of a second—

But she is learning a new thing now: light will spring her,
fixed though she is. She's already on her way.
She is escaping, little by little.
Someday that I will call *today*,
not far from now,
I'll look for her and all I'll see
will be an orange glow, like sunset.
She will have gone into light.

ACTING CLASS

I have to say to myself a little sternly:
forget the girl in the coat with the red hood
looking at her reflection in the window
of the subway car as it careens
through the dark tunnel, the girl thinking,
*This could be the opening
of a movie! A girl in a coat with a red hood,
looking at her reflection
in the subway window. The camera
follows her as she gets out
at Grand Central, walks with the crowd
toward the shuttle.*
                         Forget the girl
freezing in the wind down Bank Street,
going to acting class with nothing in her mind
but a picture of a girl in a red coat,
going to acting class.

BROOKLYN, BROKEN *Summer 1978*

We said we were in hell. I think we laughed.
The plaster felt hotter than our skin.
The bar below was fumigating.
Half-poisoned roaches staggered up our walls.
The narrow hall we'd painted red
was like a rifle barrel as the shot is fired.

I made tabbouleh for the friend you hadn't seen since college.
The evening stumbled on—heat, sweat, sirens, roaches.
Finally we walked him to the subway.
The air hung thick and vaporous around the streetlights,
but my mind had a cold, sharp edge.
I was the invisible one, beginning to see
that really I was real. Your friend
pushed through the turnstile,
raced for the train back to Manhattan,
waving goodbye as the doors slid shut.

The two of us walked back in silence,
climbed the brown stairs. You were the hollow hum
inside the rooms, you were the light fingers,
caressing, late in the night,
the underside of your own arm.
We lay on the mattress, sheetless,
our bodies touching nowhere.
All that night of Brooklyn heat,
the small fan blessed us like the pope—
one, then the other,
one, then the other.

WELL, COME IN, HONEY

The story was called 'Unbeknownst to Me.'
She had a sort of vision, is how it began.
It filled her with such yearning, almost like grief,
that it seemed she was in mourning
for the future she'd been meant to have—
in which she was climbing a gravel road
that curved around a hill, a tunnel through trees.
It was getting on toward dark.
She was carrying a cabbage to an elderly neighbor
in a cabin at the crest of a hill.
'Well, come in, honey,' the old lady said.

That was as far as I got, with that particular vision.
I had it on the F train to Brooklyn, where I lived then—
the landlady's mother shouting curses in Russian
out her fourth-floor window, bass rhythms
from the tavern down below vibrating against the floor
we had painted a hopeful shade of white,
I and my—what do you call it—soon-to-be-then-husband,
massaging his temples over there, heartsick
from not living in the Renaissance.

That's mean, I guess. But I was lucid by then.
No, I mean I was lurid by then. Lurid is just lucid
looking for an exit. Panic is just
the line of tightness across the chest
and another, throat to crotch,
a kind of cross.

Now, almost a lifetime later, I'm walking up a hilly road at dusk.
July already. The round straw bales left on the slanted green hill
are gold in the long wet light of evening.
The old neighbor the girl was going to see
in the blind and groping past turned out to be me,
because when my real husband—
the one who seemed delighted to welcome his life
whenever it happened to happen—
left this world for whatever happens next,
Eddie Wayne, our firewood man,
showed up at the front door
with a nice big cabbage, to comfort me.

And I was comforted. That girl on the F train
wouldn't know me now.
Well, come in, honey.

BOTTICELLI'S *VENUS*

I thought she arose from the sea. I thought she must be remembering her long hair streaming behind her, her life green and flowing, before something willed her upward out of that deep, watery world and she broke the surface.

I thought she had a past.

But no: she arose from the foam. She was nothing, or only air mixed with concussion of water, before she was this pale translucent girl, standing barefoot on the sharp, ridged hinge of a half-shell, not tipping it over and spilling into the surf, as she would have done, had she weighed anything at all. Yet the fierce figure of wind blows at her back as though he thought she had substance, as though she were a sail. She may be moving toward the abrupt shore, but it seems through—dare I say?—an error in perspective, she has already run aground. Primavera, or her sister, Earth, waits on the shore for her, flinging out a flowery drape to cover the girl or to warm her like a newborn child. The drape has stalled in midair. It seems permanent there. I doubt it will ever land.

Perhaps this girl has no future, either.

Long before, in Greece, some hard-pressed man
probably imagined her, or at least the possibility of
her, one wild night of storm, and went around telling
of the figure he'd seen, rising in the spray, luminous,
beautiful beyond what anyone had ever known of
beauty in a woman, and—oh—naked. And there was
such a passion of belief in him, and such a passion to
believe him in the ones he told, that he was believed.
The idea made the world more interesting; radiance
and joy and longing entered in. And so the story
went round—Venus had swirled up out of foam.
They called her Aphrodite—*foam-borne.*

Many years passed, and then, in Florence, Botticelli,
searching for an image of perfect womanhood who
was not the Madonna (who of course could not be
presented nude), painted a young girl, standing
casually balanced on one foot on her unstable craft.
One hand covers one breast; almost absentmindedly,
she uses her cascading ankle-length, amazingly vital
fair hair to half-veil herself. In her face is the resigned,

calm, inward look of an exile, somehow spent,
beyond all weeping, though she is very young, fifteen,
I'd say, with a bit of baby fat through the belly still.

She can't be grieving, can she? Grief requires a *before*,
and she was never anything till now. And she can't be
yearning, either, which would require a sense of the
future. She is foam, a figment. Unlike, for instance,
Vermeer's girl, pouring water, or Rembrandt's
Hendrickje, wading in a river with her skirts tucked
up—they, too, involved with water but of a more
daily kind. They come to this instant in their
unfurling lives, human women, lifted out of their
mortality and imperfection by the painter's love, but
relentless in their expectation of moving on. One
almost senses in them an impatience—if only he
would hurry, if only they could stop posing and get
on with it.

But Venus has no plans. Though everything in the
painting is in motion, she is still. This pale naked girl
on an impossible craft in a dubious sea, in a position
of precarious balance which looks nevertheless
static—an instant ago she was nothing. She cannot
put a foot on shore. She's going nowhere.

Part Three: Here is the River, Here is the Road,
Here is the Rain

THIS POEM

I want this poem to be my skeleton—
my clavicle, my rib, my anklebone,
my long spine, intricate and strong.
I want to walk it out into the throng
of creeping shapes that aim to live
my life for me. I want to give
this courage to myself.

              I want this poem
to be my final resting place, my home,
what's left of me, sharp and exact,
what I was here for, boney fact.
One day when I fall with my whole weight,
I want this poem to slam itself into my fate.

SECRET

Before I wake, the life of the world
goes on and is a secret and I am
within the secret.

Waking, I lie still. Nothing moves
except the clouds flowing across the moon,
diffusing its almost-perfect roundness
as it rises through the boughs of the maple tree.
The soft rain falls on the still leaves.
I watch the smear of light crawl up the clouds.
Then the moon breaks free for a moment
in its own clear definition.

I only watch.
I do not ask to be let in.
I am let in,
until these words come to me.

Then I am let out.

ESCAPE

Here is the river, here is the road,
the moonlit wet road, curving uphill.
Shall I go now? I have my five things.
I could go now.

Listen.
Nothing was a mistake.
Everything was
the road to here.

Once, I was nowhere.
I could go anywhere.
Anywhere seemed full of promise.
I went anywhere.
I packed my trunk.
I gave the rest away.
Just follow the road where it leads,
I told myself.

Now I think, Stay.
To escape means
to stand at the edge of the porch,
watching the rain on the road.
I learned this.

Here is the river.
Here is the road.
Here is the rain.

LAND CHANTY

Here in Kentucky, we've got time.
We're floating on its soundless boundlessness,
absence of sea our main.

This once was sea. Now on this day,
old thunder rolls downhill over the pond.
The grasses swell and swing. We cast our nets
into the bonny shoals of horseflies.
This chunk of limestone is our only anchor,
a million lives a million years ago,
compacted, dense and heavy in our clay.
We hoist it from the garden, haul away.
We're bound for better weather. We set sail,
the white sheets on the line filling with wind.

BELL OF BREATH

Snow coats the branches of old trees on North Broadway.
Sudden light strikes down, then vanishes.
It is the bell's tongue. *Now,* tolls the bell.
I have driven this road a thousand times.

The world is on fire. Secret bells in the blood ring out;
they sound the coming in and going out of souls.
I am trying to remember those I love, their faces.
I am trying to say *thank you* as I go.

The world today has been full of small bells.
Purple finches at the feeder. Fallen oak leaves,
standing on edge, moving like birds across the ground.
Starlings fly up now—great waves, parabolas of starlings
join and separate. The tree sucks them in and the sky is empty.
Then, from the top of the courthouse, another flight bursts up,
a great bell ringing back and forth: *Now! Now!*

In the night, I part my life like long grass
and step through it. What is it now that walks?
Bell of breath. I thought I would be frightened.
I am relieved. When the bell tolls,
dead is not the sound it makes,
nor the sound that rings on afterward.

Waking. Kissing. Dressing by the stove,
noticing the sun's red rim rising into low clouds,
making the oatmeal, throwing in the raisins,
reading the horoscope, drinking the coffee,
ascending the stairs…

PEEPERS IN MARCH

Peepers in March, geese flying north,
blonde dogs in blonde grass, taking the sun,
trees branching high, throwing down their first shade,
new leaves full of birds, days full of song,
slippery life slipping out of its coil,
right through our fingers, ungraspable, gone.

Love hovers around us. We don't know a thing.
But here are the peepers, here is the spring.

INEXPRESSIBLE

I want the inexpressibleness of eagles.
The great banking silence of their wings.
I'm on my knees, digging clover out of the cracks
between the path stones. It will come right back.
The tangled, thick, tenacious roots are speaking to me—
Be on the earth while you are on the earth. Hold on.

And here is an earthworm I've unearthed,
slipping across stone to get to where
he can coil up, vital and pink, and hide
under a dandelion leaf, not knowing
he's in no danger from me, not knowing
I treasure him for helping to make some topsoil
on this old clay ridge.

Earthworms are the opposite of eagles,
but also inexpressible.

And here is the wet earth itself,
made out of mown grass that fell between the stones
on top of the creek gravel and corroding cement
we set the stones in, back when we were stupid.
Here is the woman on her knees who did the mowing—
finding the shape of the stone again,
under the matted clover.

What about the inexpressibleness of *her*?
All her little words
pattering down into silence…

HERE, WITH YOU

Five nights of frost, and now a night and day
of ceaseless rain. In sullen light,
the redbud's neon bloom, brought on too early
by an easy March, fades almost as we watch
to the color of rags, leaving the sodden cedar
to say whatever April is this year.
We sit reading at the kitchen table.
I've lost all backward impulse, history's urge
to track. I don't much care how I got here.
All I am, this day, is here, with you.

But now, from the sundeck roof above us,
water flows into a crack, along a joist,
then down in quickening drops through the drywall ceiling
onto the kitchen table. We gather ourselves,
then go upstairs and open the glass doors
to see what we can do. Beyond the garden,
in the cherry trees, bearing their ruined brown hopes,
hundreds of starlings settle, passing through.
We kneel and unroll a plastic sheet
over the likely seam and weight it down
with lengths of stove wood, certain that this won't help.
The song of the first wren opens the air.

LIFE'S MOMENT

Life's moment when it comes to us
is round and lasts no time at all.

We forget, in that moment, everything
that keeps us separate and upright.
We lose our form. We go out.
Then we draw back into our strict bodies,
our bodies leashed to time.

It's almost always the earth that comes to us
this way, isn't it. Four male cardinals in the fog
among the juncos, snow defining every branch.
Or maybe sometimes someone's eyes, those rare times
when we see the spirit, as we call it,
slipping through to meet another spirit,
likewise slipping through.

Or maybe we hear it, music.
Yes, then, especially, it goes straight into us—
our bodies become that music.

The moment comes and stops us. Then it lets us go—
back to standing at the kitchen window
seeing the four cardinals among the juncos in the fog,
back to washing the pot,
back to breaking the wineglass,
because of not paying attention.

VALENTINE'S DAY

He comes bearing the dozen roses. He comes in love,
but also in bewilderment, I know,
like the other men wandering the aisles
of the grocery store this night, trying to find
the cellophane-wrapped bouquets,
trying to do what's right, trying
not to disappoint. They pay and scram,
relieved—*there, that's done! They didn't forget!*—
and bear their trophies homeward now, to love.
And here are the rose-pink roses.
I trim their stems under running water.
I don't know why—because I heard somewhere
that's what you do with roses. I lower my face
to them. I say how beautiful the color,
they even smell like roses.

            Well, February's
a twisted month, sullen, metallic,
and then a sudden purple lake
of earliest crocuses around the old house,
and the bulb called *Naked Lady* spikes up,
like hands pressed together over the head
to break the surface of the frozen soil.

I saw my face this morning, I couldn't help it,
in the mirror of the gym, the startling creases,
the bright eye—it was a face that had caught up

with itself. It didn't care if it looked good.
It didn't even care if it was happy.
It gathered physical purpose to stay alive
as long as it's alive.

                    Oh, my dear love,
my heart's already pierced with arrows.
I don't need flowers now. I only want to find,
with my own hand, my own hand, fingers pointed
upward over my head to break the surface.

But stay with me, even so, stay with me, till the end.

ANOTHER BIRDIE-IN-THE-BACKYARD POEM

He is doing the thing nuthatches do,
dithering head-first
down the trunk of the redbud,
searching for bugs
now that the seeds are gone.

'I don't want to hear
another birdie-in-the-backyard poem,'
my friend told me her friend told her.
I say: If you've seen one nuthatch, you've seen
a mystery. Over and over, always exact,
the plump, short-tailed shape
of a nuthatch. How does he know
which one he is? Isn't the universe
sometimes something? How it makes
nuthatch after nuthatch?

THE COY MISTRESS OF ANDREW MARVELL
SPEAKETH BACK

You're right, dear Andrew—we don't have world enough.
We don't have time. The winged chariot is closing in on us.
I feel it hurrying near in the small of my back.

The small of my back. Put your hands there. Hurry near.
Don't be meticulous. We're talking about deserts
of vast eternity! Oh, let's not languish.

The fine and private place is not the grave,
dear hunk of strength and sweetness.
I'm not stupid.
I already know I don't have time
to gather any rubies by any river. And, as to worms
trying my long-preserved virginity—
that's gross.

Rough strife sounds okay to me, though.
Our long love's day is zipping by.
Now, therefore, while we may—devour me.
It were no crime. The iron gates of life
swing open for us.

YELLOW MOTHS

Hundreds of yellow moths, no, thousands,
dancing up from the road
and from the long mown field of grass beyond,
cavorting, spinning.
        In the merry fluster,
two women and a little girl dance, too,
arms waving over their heads, faces raised.
There in the field, among the moths,
they twirl and prance in their baggy pants
and sloppy shirts and flip-flops.
        I want to pull over
and dance with them, that yellow confetti
flying all around, a celebration of something—
being alive, I guess.
        But I drive on, slowly,
begging the giddy moths
to fly up out of my way, to pay attention.
Some do, some don't.
When I get to the end of the moths, I speed up.
The dancing goes on, behind me.

CLOSER

They beg to be relieved of their terror, whimpering politely,
staring in grief through the glass.
Well, we all want in, don't we?
They scratch at the door. They're frantic now.
Oh, forget the freaking carpet.
Let them in.

The thunder rumbles grumbling across the sky,
the clumsy undead giant, looking for something he lost.
The band of bruised purple at the western horizon
draws like a drape across the whole sky.
The wind comes hard and wild.

Close the door fast, close your book.
Close your eyes, your leaping mind,
that rush of jaunty, clicking sounds you make
like a waterfall of shattered glass.
Hush, listen.

The trees bend down. The rain is banging
against the windows. The clanging crows fall silent.
An unmoored screened door
slams back and forth in the wind.
A sudden immense thunderclap
knocks us back, and lightning slashes down—
there goes the power.

We're on the floor now, too, our arms around
our wet and trembling dogs. Water slides down
the redbud leaves, wild out there in the dark,
rising and falling, riding the wind
as if for the thrill of it. What I feel now
is like that—grave excitement.
Here's another crack of lightning.
Closer.

OUTAGE

Three nights of candles and flashlights.

The almost-full moon floats upward now through clouds,
illuminating them as it passes. What the moon
and the cold rain and the fire and the coyotes belong to
draws close around us too. Like sleep. Thick. Vital. Silent.
It takes us in, enfolds us. We almost know its name.

When power is restored, the lights come on—
casually, as if *of course*. And that other thing
is—no, not gone—just pushed back outside
into the night.

                    In here, familiar life resumes.
The refrigerator takes up where it left off,
the heat pump bustles back to life,
and voices rip the silence,
telling the clattery news of the lit-up world.

Objects resurface, strangely unfamiliar—
even the faux-suede recliner an artifact
of some ancient civilization, revealed this way,
so suddenly and brightly—what was it *for*?

We too light up again—fragile globes
of consciousness, hunger, worry, ecstasy,
among our potholders and boots and charged devices.

We go back to being still here. Whatever *being* means.
Or *here*.
Or *still*.

Meanwhile, out there—
the moon, the wet darkness, the silence—
except for the coyote's howl.

INVISIBILITIES

Swift shadows as the restless leaves
catch a ray from the rising sun. The play of light.
A beam comes through and catches a spider's strand
dropping down slantwise about four feet
from a limb of the poplar tree to a redbud branch below.
Anchored, it stirs gently in the drift of wind
in and out of light.

Now the light climbs upward a little
and discovers, in that gap of leafy air,
dozens of strands crossing and intersecting.
Shining. The random shafts glide along
the length of one, then another,
giving away their secret,
then taking it back.

Oh, and there's the spider, the small creator,
working along one strand—
I have to look and look to assure myself it really *is* a spider,
and not another moving shard of light.

I take my eyes away to scribble those lines.
When I look up a minute later,
the sunlight has moved upward, into the leaves,
the spider's complex empire withdrawn again
into the intricate invisibilities
that hover around our life on earth.

No! One low strand still catches the shine of morning.
And there's the spider again, a flash of her,
floating in midair in the world's quick light.

57

PINE MOUNTAIN

Light came and went. Weather came and went. And
this, for a long time was forever, when forever stood
still. No—not still. The sea gathered. The sea receded,
leaving a rich mud. We come from mud.

Continents banged together. The surface in this place
was thrust upward. Water ran down along the creases
in the slope.

Something happened. Some particles coalesced in the
mud, set up a faint throbbing, and then organisms
began to move, to inch along, to swim, or to send
themselves downward, deep into the mud, probing to
find what they needed in order to push themselves up
into the air. And so the forest came. The hemlocks rose
up, the great oaks. Things came winding through the
trees. Things with wings or legs or bellies moved along
the ridge, or with fins through the ridge's waters, all
looking for what they needed, for life. Huge things,
mastodons and bison. And also things almost invisible.
All sorts of things began to be alive.

It took forever.

Then some came through on two legs. They needed
everything. They had no claws or long sharp teeth to
help them kill. They only had brains. And clever hands.

They used them to make weapons out of stone. They figured out how to make fires and cover themselves against the cold, since they no longer had fur. They needed shelter. They needed to clear places to plant corn. Some of them moved on through. Some stayed, perhaps—they didn't leave much trace.

They could come back. If this had been the place you knew when you hunted here, ten thousand or so years ago, you could come back now and know where you were. You would remember the ridgeline, the steep slabs of bare sandstone at the crest, holding the memory of creation. That long ridge has remained, unmolested, unblasted, unchanged, still itself.

The ridges of most of the neighboring mountains are gone. Blasted and bulldozed away. No human or animal could find the way back.

But on Pine Mountain's crest, I saw, almost, what they saw—millions of years around me. Of course they would know it is not as it was then. The cougars are gone. The bison are gone. The chestnut trees they knew are gone, the hemlocks severely threatened, the ash trees dying before our eyes. Still, I saw what they saw, the shape of the land—as close to forever as we're likely to get.

RUIN IS NOT THE END OF ANYTHING

God in the branches and branchlets down to the last twig,
and in the spiders scrambling out of the uprooted weeds
as they fall and in the sudden snake sliding exposed
into the long grass and disappearing.
God in the deer mouse the cat has cornered, God in the cat,
God in the torn screen, the rusted gutter,
the broken downspout, the fence rails hanging by one nail.
God in the places we forget to go.

Praise the great variety and particularity of God:
the fleabane in the last light, the frayed and flapping
prayer flags in the wind, the evening coming,
God coming out the clouded window,
God dancing with the spider and the prayer flags
and with the old ones by the pond, dancing forever
outside our time, singing *Ruin is not the end of anything.*

Through the night that rises now behind this cabin,
a man has been waiting, somewhere else, for dawn,
and the sharp curved sword that will sever
his head from his body. Oh spiders, oh flowing grasses,
oh branches of all trees, be with the man
who is beyond our rescue and ransom.
God of upheaval, God of love, God of ruin. Oh earth,
go to the man, hold him in your unruly arms.
At the sword's edge, turn him to water.
Bring peace bring peace bring peace.

Be now in the beheaded. Be in the beheader.

INDIGO BUNTING

I.

The feathers of the indigo bunting the cat killed
shine in the morning wind like broken mirrors,
smithereens. The green-black wings once scalloped
a little dip of breeze. The life wanted to fly,
the body knew how. The life went out
on breath and did not come back. The torn
blue chest had a long song it would sing.

II.

The distant high thrilled yelping in the night
means something is being taken from us—
for food, I suppose, or play: a squirrel perhaps
or some small dog cornered in the dry creek bed.
At dawn, an indigo bunting sings in the maple wood.
The cat purrs in a patch of sun. Life goes on, goes on.
We are all one thing. There's no comfort in this thought.
I'm leaving something out. I don't know what.

Part Four: The Wavering World

THE TETHERED GAMECOCKS

Down the hill a mile,
out of the sky-blue oil drums in ordered rows,
the tethered gamecocks sing for the sun of their day.
Their rough merriment rises
and bursts over the horizon of their lives,
out of the long rolling darkness of that time
when wings and air belonged to them,
when they strode forth in majesty
and ruled the roost.

What do they have now?
Feed and red rage, the need to kill,
they can't remember why.

And to crow.
The sun comes.
It rises in them.
They can't help crowing.

SEEING RED

Red, red, red—little monomaniac. His one idea's a
dumb idea. Demented cardinal, careening full-tilt
at our kitchen window to attack the loathed other.
You'd think after the first twenty times he'd learn:
pane of glass, pain of glass. No. He cannot overcome
himself. He sees red. A trigger for testosterone.

Cardinal shape in that alcove of strangeness, dim
intimation. He gets the message. It flurries in his
nerves. *Enemy. Rival. Interloper.* He has no choice.
He attacks himself. He'd kill himself if he could.
He'll never figure it out.

He thinks the blow he feels each time is the other
one, winning. He cannot make the connection.
Furious, repelled, he somersaults onto the sill to
peck and peck and peck the unbreakable barrier:
you bastard, you bastard!

Finally, desperate for him and for ourselves, we
hang newspaper on the outside of the window
toward which from the lilac bush he launches his
attacks. This stops him for a time. He wanders,
robbed of purpose, branch to branch, until he spies
another interloper in the upstairs window—he
rushes toward his destiny, joyful and fierce. There
can be no end so long as there are windows.

Oh cardinal, you scrap of territorial will and lust
all through you to protect what's yours. You would
enter with no reflection that mystery looming
inward—shining, muted, almost invisible—to
defend the real tree you know, and all you call your
own. Oh cardinal, listen! It is nothing! It is the
shadow of your own dear world, your very self,
you fly at. Settle down.

BOWLS

Smooth, round, remarkably uniform
and gently luminous are the skulls
of the slaughtered Cambodians
lined up in rows on wide shelves,
many hundreds, like inverted bowls
waiting to be glazed and fired.

Where are the hopes, the bright ideas,
the memories of dreams
that filled each one, the purposes
of mornings these skulls woke to,
once, when the sun meant anything
but the metallic glare of power
mixed with abstract rage and righteousness?
Where are the thoughts they had
before their only thought was terror?
Terror is what remains—not theirs. Our own.

Their terror disappeared with their blood
into the ground or into water, perhaps.
That swift evacuation made a whirring sound
in their ears like wings, a rustling sound
like wind, and then only a white lifting-away
from time, from that moment when
a sharpness tore into their treasure
of flesh, as the pain at last, or so we hope,
drained away with their blood and life.

Let these skulls which once held lives
be bowls for us. Turn them over
so that they can hold at least our breath,
the breath of the ones still breathing,
here on the edge
of the next thousand years or so.

THE BARKING DOGS

'Simplify the world till it becomes
two white moths spiraling upwards over the stones,'
I tell myself.
        The world comes barging back,
banging pot lids, bellowing its song:
It's all mixed up. Yes, it's all mixed up.
The old grab bag, the jumble and mess,
the forty-two dead again in Mosul,
the moths, the bills, the hills, the budding lilies,
the squeaking door, the leaking roof, the nest
of almost fledgling sparrows on the porch,
knocked down, I'm sure, by our own murdering cat,
one baby still alive. We put the nest
back in the tree.
        The cat will come again.

The drought, the shouting geese, the sudden rain,
the tiny enlarged node, the sparrows
who built the nest and fed their young
all day for weeks, the hatchling in the nest,
tonight alone with its three murdered siblings.
The full moon, the barking dogs, the cat,
the neighbor's pony, now rummaging through
my bed of early kale.

Oh my dear, there's better and there's worse.
The two of us together—
        what comes next?

EASTER MORNING

The sycamore in its clutter of limbs
spins in brightness down in the draw
like a skeleton dancing, twirling and clicking
its ancient bones.

The great force and mystery gathers itself,
springs out of the redbud's smooth brown branch—
flamboyant, fluorescent, a miracle
we've come to expect.

Meanwhile, the finches, in new yellow plumage
frolic and squabble over their seed
like mean Easter eggs. And now the geese
start heading for home.

The season of ice slinks into the ground
muttering threats, leaving behind
a wreckage of woods and a few frozen pipes
to remember it by.

HERE, IN SILENCE

On PBS, the kids who'll never again become available to us
have been going by in their fast smiles all this time.
All this time, I've been looking at their lips,
which won't be kissed again. Beautiful smooth lips,
uncertain nervous lips, noble for-posterity lips,
back-alley lips, lips that have practiced a sexy Elvis sneer,
regular twenty-year-old, stretched-for-the-camera,
gleeful lips, kissing, as their day and every other day
they were supposed to have blew up around them,
the winter mud on some mountain
they didn't even know the name of.

They didn't know what else to do—
the electronics department at Sears,
working on straight commission, nobody buying
in that economy. They paused in front of the recruiting kiosk.
It seemed like something they could do.
Something to be proud about. Excited about—
the challenge, the steady salary, the adventure.
Something new and definite. Heroic, even.
Some thought, I guess, that if you loved your country,
well, it was time to step up.

Karzai? Who was he? Baghdad, they knew, was bad.
Kabul? A place where whistling in the street, they'd heard,
was once a crime, until our guys came in
and got rid of the guys who beat up women.
And don't forget Bin Laden and the Towers
and don't forget the WMDs
over there in Saddamville.

And don't forget, either, the guns,
and the chance to get the bad guys in your sights.

Someone ought to write the alternative history,
the one about not going there. Where would we be now,
say, if Gore, if the Supreme Court…

Oh, these forks in history's path. Who knows?
I only know the dead kids on TV.
Sure, there was a chance
they'd be the ones, but they played cards to pass the time,
kept their Facebook pages current—
and here in silence, here in silence, here in silence, are eleven more.
I hope they all were flat-out kissed sometime.
What if they never were, what if all the good stuff
was still ahead of them and then
they had to drive their Humvee into a landmine?

Now we have before us, as we set the table for dinner,
Irving Trent from Indianapolis, his body,
once so knuckle-cracking ready, jittery for life,
for whatever—his tall, stilled bones in a long box now.
His parents accept the flag presented to them
at his grave. That flag. That photo on TV.
(He looks so brave and capable, with his big ears and shining eyes
and hopeful, kissable lips.) That's it, for Irving Trent,
who gave his life for—what?

The graves of dead kids, out to the horizon. Tell me.
For what?

HOPE

Hope is the thing with feathers, our dear Emily said,
and I've had that kind of hope, standing at the window
thinking *maybe, maybe, and someday and God! What if—?*
I spent my youth hoping. The feathery part was when,
for a moment, I believed. That thrill, fluttering upward,
stomach to heart.

But what if there were no window?
What if there were only a tent flap,
opening onto rows and rows of other tents,
and you were there, waiting
and hoping, with your three thin children
and the knapsack of clothes you were able to carry out
and your husband, if he had not been blown up, or murdered,
and your daily allotment of lentils,
and everything you knew as life bombed out,
lost, left behind—your little house, your good dog.
Maybe your parents, left behind also,
will have enough food to give a little to him.
Oh! don't think of them now, don't!
Your cooking pots, your friends,
the pretty things you treasured in your other life,
the very water that once ran freely
through your days, for tea, for washing dishes,
for bathing your children and your own body,
which once gave you such pleasure.

What would hope feel like then? The thing with edges, maybe,
serrated by grief and fear and anger, like a knife sawing through
a loaf of hard, dry bread. I wish you fortitude
and desperate determination.
I hope you find some yoghurt and an onion,
and that you have a way to cook the onion
in oil till it caramelizes, the way I've learned to do
from my Middle Eastern cookbook. And that Allah
or God or luck or some kind of human kindness
sends you some garlic and a little cinnamon.
I hope, though the feathers are surely gone,
that you don't lose hope. Let hope be sharp as steel.
Here, from my morning table in Kentucky,
are my thirty dollars. I hope you find your way
to a kind place.

HOW IT COMES ON

See how the world comes out of the fog.
See how it comes on and gathers
as though nothing had changed,
the world still here, almost the same.

This is the way the world delivers its treasure—
the pale undersides of our two dogs' tails
like flares running before us
up the almost invisible path.

One leaf, then another, flashes on the branch.
The addled, wandering wasp tumbles upside-down
on a fallen weed, the spider's strand

glistens across our way—all things
as we come near them moving into light,
our bodies toiling up the hill,
the bothered turkeys taking to the trees.

The light burns through and gives this day to us
and we are burning as we go.

LETTING GO

Little scooter of fur and flesh, scouting fast
in darkness here and there—clever feet,
quick-panting belly, tiny intricate skull,
busy brain. A bit of cheese right there before her.
The astonishing metal crack, the blast of pain,
the almost-killing shock.

I found her in the morning, still alive,
one hind foot caught. She tried to crawl away,
dragging the trap.
I closed one hand around her soft weight,
lifted the bar with the other. She never moved
as I carried her, cupped in both hands,
through the cool spring morning
to the compost heap. I felt her heartbeat
against my palms.

I knelt and set her down. Freed, she did not move.
We faced each other. I felt large.
She held me steady in her shining, upward gaze.
Not supplication, no. Her eyes were calm, alert—
curious, I'd almost say,
waiting for whatever would happen next.
'You can kill me now. If that's what you want to do.'
We stayed this way a little time.
Then I turned my eyes aside, and she took her only chance.
She burrowed down, dragging her broken foot,
under the orange peels and egg shells, into the rich world
of going back. I watched her disappear.

Later that day, behind a gnawed-up roll of toilet paper
on the linen-closet floor, I found the nest—
a cradle really, extravagantly soft, scooped out
to hold the four transparent babies.

I didn't know what to do. I lifted the nest in both hands
like something to be blessed and carried it, too,
out to the compost heap. I hoped she'd find it.
I kept the cats inside.

That evening, when I looked again, the nest
was there, intact. The babies all were gone.

And I would live to set more traps.
I knew I would.

STAY

Plaintive and desperate, the coyotes tonight
are begging the moon,
the whole round solemn perfect fact of it,
to stay, to stay right there, high over the hill.

It does not stay.

Before any mouth or breath, in the first great flood
of emptiness, already the moon was drifting
up through stars and flying clouds,
then falling out of sight at the western edge,
already the moon was turning in and out of earth's shadow,
earth's darkened sky the moon's great stage.

There was no audience.

But then, silent ages later, in darkness and light,
things began to move, to hiss and grunt and roar,
and before we came to what we now call words
some creature must have noticed
where the moon came up and set,
and how it crept along the east and west horizons,
a little further to the north or south each day,
till, reaching a certain point,
it turned and started back the other way,
a noticing that took in more than *now*—
a first remembering, and so, a first prediction.

Our slow pendulum. The tick and tock of time began.
Rising, falling, waxing, waning, losing, gaining.
'Many moons ago,' we said,
when finally we said anything—

Eternal turning, returning,
as the earth turns round the sun.
We came to know the moon is bound
to the deep core of our earth. Its looping orbit
is only its desire to fly off, free.
We've harnessed something wild.
But it cannot escape earth,
any more than earth can escape the sun.

These grave attachments.

Even now, when we've been there,
planted our flag and scraped up samples
of its soil to study, even now,
such mystery.

Oh, moon—you have your strong force, too.
You rule earth's tides and pull life up out of the seed.
You rule earth's creatures as earth rules you.
We have you and then lose you, over and over.
In your fullness, our mares foal,
our women bleed, our witches dance,

our murderers feel their need like sex.
The doors of Bedlam fly open,
let loose their lunatics. Sleep slinks away.

Oh, howl like the coyotes for the moon
up there above the winter hill,
in its perfect moment of illumination—
it lasts only an instant
before the shadow of our earth
begins again to take her light away.

LIKE THE WEATHER

The seeping away of darkness, the light gathering color
as it opens, each single leaf, each blade
alive in light, as light looks for something else
to land on—the pokeberries shining in their deep color,
the morning glories translucent, God going in one side
and out the other, drunk. Leaves stir in the wind,
leaves send out their two-sided message: *We are alive,
we are becoming light. We fall like light.*

The unfurling then of the weather, visible, invisible,
across the large sky. And underneath the weather,
our lives unfurling, flying off, flapping into
and out of the light, visible, invisible,
and then, like the weather, gone.

WAVERING

The dawning sunlight as it finds the water
in the dog's metal bowl
throws its wavering reflection
onto the clouded glass door.
The cherry trees in the back woods
are white with both bloom and snow
and green with coming leaves.
Male finches in their sudden yellow plumage
flash in and out of the boughs.

Oh beautiful, uncertain, wavering world.

Sometimes I know that someday
I will be gone from all I know,
my earthbound life.

I thought the earth would stay.

But in my flare of life I've seen
treasured pieces of the world
fly off. The litany of loss—
honeybees, ash trees, rainforests,
coral reefs, Monarchs, mountain ranges.
Giraffes and glaciers,
elephants and chimpanzees.

Loss is all around us. Something else
is winning, for a while, before it loses too.
Gone is the gong that sounds now,
as I drink my coffee and watch, for a while,
the finches in the cherry trees,
the light rising like smoke.

MARRIAGE IN THE MIDST OF THINGS

Oh, the cricket sings in the heat duct, loud he sings
the only song he knows, two notes through the night.
Over and over he sings the difficult thing,
that a cricket in the house might mean good luck,
but a cricket in the heat duct is a goner.
Fast, fast he sings the urgent, desperate news,
as many times as he can in his one short life,
while the scatterbrained storm gathers itself across
the midnight sky, with lightning flashing and cracking
in every direction at once. And now the thunder
rolls down wide circling stairs that lead to us.
In the flare of the random lightning the ancient elms
fling their limbs upward, wild against the sky,
against all odds still here, still with us, still
in the midst of things alive.

Now the dead bough crashes
down on the picnic table, not on us.

The torrent sheets the screen, the sump pump roars.
We're riding it out in our house, though one of us
sleeps through it and—amazingly—does not hear
the thunder or the cricket, let alone
the drenched cat pawing against the glass door,
then clawing his way out of the old blue towel,
flying through darkness onto our new white chair.

Oh, the cricket, the elm, the rain, the cat, now washing
his feet so calmly, the sleeper and the watcher,
the rolling bed of the world, the marriage of all
in spite of all.
In spite of all.
Amen.

Part Five: Joy Dogs

A FLASK OF THIS

The old lopsided hula hoop of time
swings round   swings round   swings round
the slowly shimmying sun.
Who are we, my love, taking this sliding ride,
careening through our uneven days and nights?
Here's fall again, our wedding month.
The slanted light comes back to speak
of what we will be missing later on—
the long light longing just ahead of time
for what is not yet gone, for itself, in fact,
drifting through early haze, touching the spires
of firestalk, the dragonfly sunning its wings
on a rock, the breeze, the gentle, living air.
We need a flask of this to see us through,
to pass to one another as we go,
to help us through the iron days to come,
to make us drunk.

Oh, drunken globe of the earth in your wobbly course,
nothing is lost forever, is it? We'll come round
to this again. This day will come again,
and we'll be in it.

TIGHTROPE

The moment of lifting,
of standing on one foot as the other
is in motion past it—
                            that is *now*.

The moving foot finds the rope again, settles.
The rope gives a little, swaying, responding
to the careful, placed weight,
as the body realigns itself
and gathers its intention
to bring what's now the back foot
forward.
                            Oh balance, balance!

The oxygen tank exhales, sighing
like a person who has cried herself to sleep.
                    Then silence,
                    then the sigh,
                    through the night.

The recliner is his world now. I lie on the couch
the next room over
so that I will hear him
when he calls—*Dearest*—out of the night.

I go to him. We hold each other as we can.
                    The past, I used to call it,
                    when it went from me
                    into the streaming air.

I place my fingers on his fragile wrist.
I count and lie: 'No, it's only skipping a little,
no more than mine.' His thin, articulate fingers,
arthritic knuckles. His wild white eyebrows
and sudden laugh: 'This is absurd.'

The oximeter, the tank,
the pure oxygen of *now*. Oh love.

Once, waiting for Angela,
we sat on a bench in the Place de la Contrescarpe.
Three men got out of a little Renault
with their instruments—
a bass, a sax, a guitar.
They set up across the street, began a riff:
A turn to the right,
a little white light.

We're out of history now.
We have one step, then another.

That's all we ever had.
We don't look down.

LIKE TALL GRASS BENDING

Go now, before the world goes still, before
the cicadas begin their incessant song of time
when time gets slow and heavy. Go now, dear heart,
while there is still a breeze, a few irises, the roses in a flush.
You want to stay, I know, for love—the round table,
the creek, the field of light through which your life has rolled.
But you've had the best of it. Today, the lug of moisture
in the air lures us with false promises of rain,
the hope of a few more high bright crystal days
like the days we've had. But, since there's no relief
in sight, turn now, open your hand, let everything
you've held so close fall free. Give your hand
to whatever takes it now.

Go like tall grass bending. It is too soon,
but I will follow in a few more seasons.
The rest are waiting for us in the wind.

CONVERSATION

'You stay with me,' he said.

'I will. I'll stay right here. I won't leave you.'

'No. Come with me, I mean.'

'I can't, you know. I have to stay on *this* side till it's time for me.'

'Oh,' he said. Then in a moment, 'What do you think it will be like?'

'I don't know. Nobody knows. Like Paris, maybe. Maybe like a long, good sleep, with wonderful dreams. Or no dreams. And then you wake up somewhere, rested.'

'I hope it will be like here.'

'Yes. Like here. That's what I hope, too. Wait for me, if you can.'

'But stay with me. All right?'

'Yes. I'll be right here, the whole way, as far as I can go.'

Stay with me.

Come with me.

Wait for me.

Stay with me.
Stay with me.

STILL HERE

It was his last day in the body he had then.
Earth's longest light had passed three days before
and now we were falling back the other way.
He came and went. He opened his eyes. He laughed.
'Seven obituaries,' he said. And then,
'That was a joke. Did you get it?'

A little past midnight, he was gone.
I sat with what was left of him for hours
while the nurse from Hospice (thinking, I suppose,
I needed distraction) told me everything
about her trip to Florida, about her daughter,
the straight-A junior high school student.
He would have known how to stop her, kindly, frankly.
He wasn't there. It should have been easy to say,
'I need to be alone now.' I couldn't do it.
I nodded. I smiled. I tried to think of her voice
as if it were water. It went on and on—
our two bodies, his and mine,
like rocks it flowed around.
It finally occurred to me to tell her she could leave.

There'd been a mix-up, it turned out,
between the various dispatchers.
Two men arrived at last, at three a.m.
They carried his body, zipped now in a black bag,
down the path.

I followed, barefoot,
through the wet grass to the edge
of the road, and watched as they
slid the bag into the cargo space
of a late-model SUV
doing service as a hearse
and drove away. I didn't care.
He wasn't in that body anymore.
They could do whatever they liked with it.
He was in the dark new day all around me,
in the air touching my skin. The scattered stars
were bright in the high quiet sky.

Now, after a day of rain, I walk out into the woods.
Oh, tender earth!
Still here, wet and green, moving in the wind.
The trunks of trees stand tall and shining
in the late, slanted light.

But the dogs have found something alive
inside a rock pile. They've taken up positions
on either side, commanding whatever's
in there to come out. Some little terrified thing…

NOW YOU ARE LEAVES

Now you are leaves
taking the wind,
whipped backwards,
silver in your flailing,
helpless.

Now you are sudden and alone,
one leaf, wild and particular
against the heavy stillness
of all other leaves,
intimate, urgent,
moving in a single private fluster
or perhaps a jubilation of the air.

Now you are patient, tireless,
attentive all the gentle day
to the way the leaf of you
slides over another leaf,
or over a slender reed,
moving in and out of light,
as tentative, exploratory
as the circling above you
of two white moths.

And when another weather races in,
and rain comes on and thunder rolls
downhill across the sky at midnight,
you are the questing leaves
of the morning glory vine
finding the window at last.
You hold against the screen,
you send small messages—'Hello.'
'Goodbye.' 'Dearest.'
'Thank you.'

And now you are a random
soft stirring all around me.
The leaves of you
answer the morning breeze,
like birds awakening,
calling to one another,
here then there.

DOWN THERE

At first I thought your urgent spirit could move now
into a baby somebody loved
and would never desert, or into a garden
like heaven, into a bird
in a garden, into that place you always sought
where everything is one.

            Then feathers were floating down
wherever I went—feathers of finches, cardinals,
indigo buntings, tanagers, downies, jays.
Dozens and dozens of feathers.
I gathered them, I kept them near me,
little vases of feathers.
Leaves in the path shaped like hearts, redbud leaves
where no redbud grew. A red, heart-shaped paper clip
on the dining room table from who knows where.
A water-stained valentine magnet beside the road,
You are always in my heart. I stuck it on the refrigerator,
thinking, 'You're working with what you can find.
It's sort of a game, you're telling jokes,
to comfort me.' A bus token, 1917,
from the Lexington Transit Company,
which your grandfather ran, buried under leaves
on the porch I'd swept a thousand times before.
A camera, for God's sake, that the dogs dragged up
from somewhere, its archive full of photographs
of one particular horse. A bouquet
of deflated pink and blue balloons,

their ribbon streamers tangled in weeds
way out in the furthest field. 'It's twins.' Messages.
Miracles. I gathered them. I kept them.
I thought you were trying
to stay with me. Maybe you were.
I was trying to stay with you.

Later, I thought that if I in my gravity let go,
you might be free to rise, a pink and blue balloon.
I thought I should let go. What I know of you,
I know, is over—quick blue eye,
jaunty step, luminous, smooth bald head.
But your absence seems dense and anchored,

and when I let go, I am the one rising.
A translucent membrane holds around me.
What if it breaks now? To be so fragile
and so full of light makes me dizzy
and afraid.

                    Down there,
a woman moves, feeds another log into the fire.
Lame dogs sleep on their cushions.
Meager, directionless snow wanders down
toward the frozen ground of a new year.
It's morning. I can see it all
from where I am.

JOY DOGS

The joy dogs wake and stretch, roll over
to get their bellies scratched,
then race away, tracking a scent
that comes to them on the wind,
and now they're barking
at the edge of the woods, barking
gladness of squirrels, rabbits, little things to chase
and kill, if they can—the oldest thing
they know, the deepest in their blood,
the least to second-guess,
although there is shouting that they sort of hear
coming from the one who feeds them,
the belly-scratcher, who wants them to turn away
from what their lives most urge them on to do,
catch up with (corner, snap their jaws at last
around) the furry throb. They're electric with it.
They bark up the tree, delirious.

I give up on them and turn away,
disgusted. I've had it with *élan vital*.

It's not spring, anyway, just March, the sorry end
of a bad winter. Each day
has seemed leaden, permanent—
a week with ice on every branch,
then gray, dripping silence,
a narrow escape, a little thaw

before the next big snow, and then
a string of days with highs of ten,
fierce wind, tornados down the road,
thunder, sleet, one day of sun
for every six of rain. Afternoons,
I trudge across the frozen grass
for another wheelbarrow-load of wood,
or, early in the morning, for the paper,
to read about the street fighting in Basra,
the stock market down again, the glaciers
sliding, everything sliding away.
Then two dogs, two cats, one gloomy woman,
all hunkered down in the living room
around the stove.

But now: the metallic, waiting world.
Things coming up, coming out,
daffodils in the dull air. A week
like a slow sea voyage, fogbound,
but inside the fog, a change of light.
The valley reasserts itself, the folds of hill,
the single far-off light tucked into a crease.
A livid pink sunset dissolves into purple dark.
The black cat sleeps in the gentle lap
of dear old steadfast, loving Raggedy Ann,
from when I was five—I want to be more like her.

At dawn, a frail beginning takes a flying leap
out into gray, uncreated time, hopeful,
heedless. The joy dogs rise up,
give themselves a shake, remember their legs,
begin to sniff the air. I rise up myself
and wander out to greet them,
in spite of all I know, or by now can guess.

Those runaround dogs. Those barking fools.

THE RIM OF SOMETHING

The rain came down steadily all day
like a gray-suited banker on his way
to work. Came down like a column of figures.
I'm not lonely. I have a chance here
to know who's doing the talking,
since it's only me.
(Don't say, 'It's only me.')

The life I say I lead has led me
to the rim of something.
The rim is slippery at its sloping edges
because of all this rain, and so I slide
into the fast air of downwardness.
I have a tomato cupped in my hand,
cool-skinned, weighty, ripe.

That was just a little pre-dream dream.
In the real dream, as I fall,
I am nursing a baby. There are no sides,
only this narrow tube of falling.
I hold the baby close against me.
A voice comes out of the abyss.
'Nothing doing,' it says.

I am not doing the talking.
I hold the baby close against me.
We are falling fast into another thing—
goodbye to cats on the bed and words

and light and towels in the dryer that
want to be taken out and folded
and whatever I remember of the life I led
that led me to the edge, to whatever is
where no blood is, no pulsing, faithful heart.

What then? I hold the baby close.
There is no baby.

WHEN I WAS HERE

After some weeks away, I'm home.
I kill the engine and sit waiting.
Soon the dogs wander up from somewhere
behind the house, through the garden,
in the afternoon's long-winded heat.
They welcome me with casual friendliness.
They're pretty sure they know me.
I step out, into my old world,
my place, and see it for an instant
with a sharp halo around it,
not so much *still here* as *gone on*—
things green and overgrown,
one dog a little thinner and more ragged
than when I left, the native
hibiscus in full bloom,
an edge of strangeness
flooding backward
toward the house where,
when I saw it first,
a little tarpaper tenant house back then,
I heard the future—shouts and music—
rolling down the red tin roof,
and all the past flows into
this one hinged moment
before the place closes around me
and I unload my suitcase, get the mail.

Would it be sad to come back from the dead?
To see the way the world keeps moving
away from you? The stones around here
are full of fossils. I've lifted stones, I'll tell you,
in my time, to build a fence, a path. Dogs
don't do history. They don't know *then*.
I have come back, and soon
they don't remember I was gone.

I keep remembering how I was
when I was here.

FALLING BACK

This is the day of falling back. I'm wandering
ankle-deep through fallen oak leaves
till the slanted light falls and then night falls
out of nowhere. I fall
asleep, I dream an old lover
wants to help me cross the street.

At four a.m., the eastbound planes
start falling slowly through the net of branches—
maybe they're heading toward New York.

Do you remember…

A dark wing fans the air around me
into light again. Crows in the wind
against pink fog.

I'm writing this in my plan book.
I haven't had a plan since October 8th.
I guess I'm losing hold. Sometimes my life
seems like a glint of brightness,
falling through fog. Then memory lifts,
disperses, leaving the sharp-edged, only world,
timeless. Here is the hour
I've gained. Accept it,
in kindness, as a kind of kindness,
as grace, a threshold, a crossing.
Not losing hold. Not falling. Holding.
Holding still.

SEPARATION

I dreamt I was at some gathering—many rooms.
I was alone. We'd lost touch. We weren't
together any more. Someone told me
he was in Chicago now, working
with a partner on a project—a black and white
installation at some museum.

And then I saw him,
walking along a wide Chicago street.
He was himself.
I was so glad to see him,
even from that distance.
Himself, restored to what he'd been
before the illness took him—
straight, intent, in a maroon cotton shirt,
the sleeves rolled back,
and jeans, of course. He lifted up
onto the balls of his feet with every step,
the way he did, happy, I think, deep
in deliberations
with a man in a trim gray suit.
Full of plans.

     All day this sinking strangeness.
His life going on without me. Without me.

FALLOW

Sometimes this is the spirit's color.
Quiet. A field in winter.
The fallow deer, after her fast leaping

away from the guns, curls into herself
and rests in the deep woods,
safe for a while, hidden inside
the color of fallen leaves,
the ancient, waiting color,

before the other color stirs,
as the handy roots reach in the dark
for moisture. They gather it
toward new life, now pushing upward.
The dead grass gives itself
to the rain and is carried down
a little at a time to nourish
what is alive now,
busy and shining,
waving in the breeze,
green.

SECOND WINTER

Now I begin to know who I am once more.
I face the facts. That's what January's for.

The merry, jingling season is behind us,
the celebration of the hopeful claim
that light can still somehow beat back the dark.

It's been a cold advance so far this year.
Sometimes, the clouds clear off, and hard blue sky
reveals itself as the temperature drops. The sun
strikes crystal light over the snowy ground.
Then the stars shine down from their high distances,
aloof, remote. Nothing to do with me.

Down here, I have my fire, my books, my dogs.
Some wine. Some soup. And music. And deep sleep,
almost like hibernation.

                    Early this morning,
I stood on the porch, holding three logs for the fire,
and heard wild geese high overhead, going north
through rolling fog, crying to one another
as they flew. I couldn't find them.

Enclosed now, I live inside myself
through short, gray days. This isn't bad.
The brutal intimacy of ice is what I fear.
February and March loom over the hill
in their hunched shapes, like henchmen in gray suits.
But all this dismal day, soft rain, not snow, has fallen.
I'm safe, for now. I'm home.

CONSERVANCY
Elegy for Paula Dunaway Merwin

I don't remember where we were headed, that raucous
Manhattan night. Jerry was at the wheel, shouting jolly
fuck you's out the window at the cabbies who kept trying
to cut in front of him. Diane was riding shotgun, head
ducked, hands braced against the dash. The other four of
us were crammed into the back. Jim was pressed tight
against me, yelling, *For God's sake, Jerry, slow down*, as we
clattered and swerved our way down Seventh. William
was holding Paula in his lap. What I remember, aside
from terror (we might all have been killed that night—
there's a thought), is the lights, the way they drifted over
their two calm faces. They were in some radiant, private
place, and not on Seventh Avenue at all.

Jim and I married that fall, she and William at the turn to
the new year. Diane died, a few years after she and Jerry
split up. He found—oh, lucky life—Anne-Marie. Jim
died. I went on living where we had always lived.

I guess you could say we were headed here, to this place
where we were sitting together, Paula and I, in the
long-lit evening, on the low stone wall surrounding the
pair of tombstones she and William had, without drama,
caused to be erected in a grassy clearing near to the
house—just in case the alternative treatment she'd
pursued (and really, as she sensibly pointed out, what
choice did she have?) did not allow her to stay in the
heaven she and William had patiently coaxed out of the
once-exhausted soil there—the great palm garden at the

northern edge of the island, on the ridge sloping to the stream that ran steeply to the sea. The kona wind of bright evening air was shuffling through the palms.

'Paula,' I ventured hesitantly, 'I think I never saw two faces so luminous with love.'

She laughed. 'We were in some kind of alternative reality—out of our minds, I guess you'd have to say.'

'That was at the very beginning, wasn't it?'

'There was no beginning,' she said quickly, quietly.

Engraved upon the tombstones, after the business of their names and dates of birth, the other, relentless dates to be filled in later (not much later, as we both knew very well)—the simple, spare words, *We were happy here.*

She drove me to the airport the next morning. We knew we'd never see each other again. Of course we didn't say so. 'Bye,' she said. 'Bye,' I said. I didn't want to cry. 'Thank you. Thank you for everything.' We hugged, and then I wheeled my carry-on to Security. I turned to wave, knowing as I did so that she would already be gone— I imagined her getting in her car, turning on the ignition, heading up the Hana Highway toward home.

ISLAND
for W and P

After the shadows moving like leaves over the old pink quilt,
after the doors opening and closing in the wind,
after the havoc of leaves and then the hushed rain,
the dripping dusk, our careful steps on the wet stone path,
after the thrush's clear, inquiring song
and the treadle of little rice birds in the palms,
comes the silence that sweeps us under
and all we were born into
sprays outward with the wave's concussion
against the red cliff,
the bright explosion of the spirit
into the clear and infinite space
between our first and last names.
Life, life, we call it,
calling to it in that instant
as it goes.

SWEET JUICY LIFE

The flighty turkey lumbers upwards.
In his dreams, he's a hawk,
scoping out the possibilities, swooping
down in casual maneuver, swerving
back up with something juicy
in his beak.

        No, that's not right.
In his dreams he's always a turkey.
He wants to be a turkey forever,
lurching and sauntering up the hill,
peacefully foraging little grains and bugs.
It's only panic like a bullet in his brain
that makes him ever leave the ground.
He loves the ground. Sudden concussion,
stumble of weight in the air—what would you call it?
You wouldn't call it flying. Just fleeing,
flurrying upwards to hide
in the branches, wanting,
like every living thing, to live.

        It's all the same.
Life, what's ours—the trees, the man,
the rain, the pancakes every Sunday,
the Sundays slipping by.
And clumsy, lumbering hope—
hope not to lose.

We don't know anything.

'When you're dead, you're dead,' my mother said.
She was Bohemian, practical and grim
from all those centuries of serfdom. Trying
to get to the truth, there at the end. To face
the facts. The heavy turkey of the spirit.
Keeping its head down,
clutching its earthbound life.
Still, she had Jesus on the wall—

Jesus, her good hawk. There was still a chance
that he'd glide down and grab her,
swing her upwards to meet all that she'd lost—
Mikey, the boy she'd loved when she was twenty,
her trust in her husband, her old Chicago life,
her brothers and sisters arguing and shouting. Up there,
they'd gather round the piano, they'd all have wings.
They'd sing their barbershop hosannas.
And none of them would ever die again.

But probably it would be turkeys all the way—
sweet juicy life, as long as there was life.
Sweet juicy seeds and bugs.
And then that fumbling,
turkeyish last flapping
off into the trees.

LITTLE LEASTS

Don't think of this as a journey.
It's just a ride.
You are the destination.
Where you are now
is where you were going.

And now, where you were then
is gone. And you are here,
in your blue sweats,
holding onto the handle
of the refrigerator door,
while all around you,
everywhere, forever,
galaxies and light-years
careen away, putting an end
to any notion you might have had
of distance.
                    Long ago, they say,
two nothings struck against each other,
triggering, eventually—
I mean *eventually*,
billions of what we now call years,
though then it was all one time—
along with Mars and Uranus
and a bunch of other dust,
this world of solid, amazingly particular things,
this world of little *leasts*: the striped moth floating,

wings out, in the dishwater, still alive.
You catch it on a table knife and carry it outside,
slide it carefully onto the picnic table,
where it flutters its wet wings
in the sun for a moment,
then gathers itself and tries to fly,
but falls. You set it right side up
and leave it to do or die.

Life flashes. Light comes. You receive it.
Dark comes. You sleep. Time touches your eyelids.
Your moments are held together
by filaments of self.
                              I almost think
there is no self. Only the handle
of the refrigerator door. Only your hand
upon it.

Whoever you are, you accident,
you incident of bones and skin and veins,
of hunger and memory and love,
set down in this strange little world
of minute intricacies—
                              oh, whoever you are,
open the door, see what is in there
that would be good to eat.

LANDING

As we glide down the radar beam,
as we break through the clouds,
a forward-moving line of tiny lights,
far down, comes clear. The late hour,
the ordered busyness, the small, enclosed,
mysterious intentions
propelling each light forward
soundlessly through the dark. To us,
they are illuminated ants.
That must be I-64.

And now we have begun,
we're told, our final approach.
Soon the lights of Lexington
gather against the clouds.
There's New Circle Road,
Versailles Road. We see now
where we are—cars, gray and red,
slip through the night,
as our own ordinary earth
comes up to meet us.

Our wheels touch down. We are delivered,
our supply of oxygen assured.
The interior lights come on.
We check to make sure we have
all our belongings. We come
to a complete stop. We who have kept
our seatbelts securely fastened
release them now. The narrow air
fills with subdued bustle. We make our way
at last into the aisle. We pull our carry-ons
from the overheads. We wait, obedient,
patient, and finally we begin to move,
a few steps at a time, like the faithful
lined up for communion
or confession. We step through the door
into the moveable chute
that leads to the terminal.

PAST PERFECT

My red silk pajamas from the Goodwill. Two bucks.
They aren't for anyone on the outside.
They feel good against my skin.
I'll wake up in a minute.
I'm happy here in bed.
I've got new sheets—

Morning's coming in the sky now.
Creeping in. I've got my eye on it.
These red silk pajamas
would knock him out.
Oh. Would have knocked. What is that?
Past perfect conditional, I think.
Here is my pen. Here is my thought.
Now, here, all around me,
he is not here.
I am trying to say how I am. Past perfect.
Conditional. A little cold. I mean
a little old. In a taxi in New York long ago,
when I was just simple future tense,
he gave me some black silk underpants.
I do not like to write what I am writing now.
I didn't like to get black silk underpants
in a taxi. He is not here. He had this laugh
on him. Comfortable and solid.
Do you remember that laugh?

Riotous, incredulous, like, 'Who can believe
this world, this world?' But now I have my book.
I'm writing in it. I'm not quite awake.
Sometime later, night comes down again.
I'm not looking for anything now
but sleep. Thunder all around, and tinnitus
like some new kind of tree frog.
Two cats on the bed. Dogs out there
barking at the new cows on the other side
of the fence. Me in here, not frozen,
in this place right here, under my throat,
where I used to cry and not cry.

BIRTHDAY GREETINGS

I didn't want to celebrate. I wanted more
just to acknowledge this day
that began when I opened my eyes
to the sharp shadows of bare limbs, precise and still,
cast by the rising sun through the closed white curtains.

Before I was quite awake, here came the perfect shadow
of a little bird—a chickadee, I think—falling like a leaf
and settling on the shadow of a limb.
It stayed there for a moment, looking around,
a sharp, perfect silhouette, and then flew up.
The limb shook in the aftermath, but then calmed down.
I got out of bed and pulled the curtain open
on the real October day.

I thought I'd begin by sitting quietly
and thinking thoughts like *what is the world,*
why is the world so—
                        But the carpenters
started to pound away at eight a.m.,
and it's been wham blam ever since.
These carpenters look like angels
by Giotto or someone, thin and tall
and sort of radiant. They're bringing me
the next year of my life. They've got
their sleeping bags and will camp out tonight
in the cabin, if that's okay with me. I make spaghetti,
though they say they brought enough to eat.

I'm thinking of my mother. On this same day,
long ago, when she was twenty-eight and I was zero,
she labored me into the dry world,
held me against her breast.
'A blondie. A little Swede,' she says she said.
'Where in the world did you come from?'

And then began
these strange engravings on the brain
which make what we call mind, this slow
accretion of the years—*my life,*
I call it, looking backward.

But, looking forward, what I see
is carpenters tomorrow at the break of day.

Part Six: Whatever Calls

MEDICAL QUESTIONNAIRE

*In the last three months, have you felt guilty about how
much you drink? Can you take care of yourself (eating,
dressing, bathing, using the toilet)? Are you forgetful?
How are you coping with the stress and pressure of your
life? Have you been feeling down in the dumps? How
often have you felt anxious or nervous for no reason?
Do you think of yourself as a failure? Are you afraid of
death? (Check one: Not at all, Moderately, Very) Does
the future look hopeless? Do you think you're looking
old and unattractive? Are you satisfied with your sex life?
(Check one: Never, Sometimes, Most Times, Always,
I Prefer Not To Answer This Question. If the latter, skip
to the next part). How would you rate your satisfaction
and happiness with your life? How important is it to you
to make changes to your lifestyle to improve your health?
How confident are you that you'll succeed?*

I feel guilty about how much I think.

I am always thinking. When I am not thinking,
I like it. When I am just noticing
that it's eight a.m. and where are the birds?
Where is *everything*, for that matter,
but this lashing wind?

              Is wind matter?
              Or is matter
just what is caught on the wind—

snow, ashes, germs, dead oak leaves
whirling down the hill like, like, like...

See? Thinking again. What do those dead oak leaves
whirling down the hill remind me of?
Tiny acrobats. Yes, put that down. 8:20.
Little somethings run across my brain,
not words exactly, little powdery flecks,
blown one way then another.
Uncreated matter. I don't know
what I was thinking...

Here are the birds at last.
Where were they before?
Hunkered down somewhere
in a cedar tree, maybe, against the wind.
And where are the cats? Sleeping
on the red down quilt. They won't wake up
till hunger makes them stir at evening.
(Do the cats think of themselves
as failures? Do they feel
their lives have no worth?
Are they afraid they're looking
old and unattractive?)
I would rate their satisfaction and happiness
with their lives on the basis of whether
a bit of juice from last night's
canned tuna has been dribbled over their cat chow.

I would rate my satisfaction and happiness
with my life on the basis of jelly—grape: not so happy,
plum or apricot: happy. I don't feel
down in the dumps, Doctor, but I have to admit
that there are times when the future
looks hopeless, how could it not, what with…
but look at that,
I'm drinking again.
I mean thinking again.

I can take care of myself—didn't I
just haul two wheelbarrow-loads of firewood
across the road? Don't I see my doctor
once a year? Don't I eat five servings
of this or that a day and work on my core?
As to my sex life, I've skipped to the next part. Okay?

Still, since you ask, I want to change my lifestyle.
No. I mean I want to change my life.
And, no, I'm not confident I'll succeed.
The hullabaloo in my head, you see,
makes me forgetful. I have trouble
concentrating. I feel anxious
and nervous for no reason.
Well, not for *no* reason.
Not exactly.

No, I wouldn't say for *no* reason.

TILTH

Grief is ground hard-packed by loss.
Nothing grows there. Dead ground.
But this place I'm in now has a little tilth.
Roots could maybe find a way
to ram on through, find sustenance.

The sullen purple remnants of the storm
trudge north, the sky behind
scrubbed down now to its hard-fact blue
by the industrious wind.
Ice on the edges of the deck after the rain.

The dogs at their evening feed: the old chow,
lying down, takes a bite and chews,
head lifted, surveying—contented, lordly—
his domain. The young black Lab stands gobbling,
wanting to clean his plate and get some more.

How we rush toward these images—
their dense familiarity. They hold us upright
in the mortal wind. Meanwhile, the cat
sleeps curled in a patch of sun on the old red rug.

STARTER FLUID

I leaned my forehead against the rough boards
of the barn door. Light was sliding down
fast. I flattened my hand against the weathered wood,
but I was leaving my skull.

I knew it was the starter fluid—ether.
I'd used too much, and now I was falling
through my body, but not to sleep.
Those splintery boards against my brow and hand
were the whole world. Everything else
was light rushing to dark.

But then I came to (came to what?
from what?), came back, swiftly,
to the shapes of things—trees, lawn mowers,
my own two feet in purple running shoes.
I took hold. I pulled the cord.
The motor started right up this time,
like the sudden world around me.
I put in my ear plugs, pushed my old mower,
with its loud bully singing, through the unruly
long sunlit grass of another spring.
I came to another spring.

GOD OF DOGS

In the middle of the night, I hoisted my ailing old
dog up and helped him out the door—he'd scarcely
moved for twenty-four hours. He stood for a while,
looking around—I'd hoped he'd relieve himself, but
he just flopped down again. I was afraid he was dying
(he wasn't, as it turned out, I'll tell you right now),
so I dragged the long cushion from the porch swing
and arranged myself to lie beside him. The moon was
on the wane, but still near full. My dog lay with his
eyes open, and mine were open, too. We looked at
each other, I with love and worry, he with calm trust,
I think, but maybe it was love. From time to time I
patted him. He licked my hand. I got up once and
bowed to the moon three times, then curled up on the
cushion again, my hand on his furry side, to feel him
breathe. The other dog, the rambunctious one, who
usually noses in, lay quietly, as if keeping watch, ten
feet away. I looked up at the high pale sky. The moon
and the dim stars came out of and went back into
thin clouds. The peepers and katydids made a cove of
sound, and the trees protected us a little from the road,
though I was worried a car might pass and someone
might think I was dead. Or crazy.

Somewhere else on earth, people were hanging their laundry on lines in refugee camps. People in Italy were beginning to stir. Cambodians, fishing all morning from slender boats, were getting ready to head back to shore. A young girl in Baghdad was strapping on her explosives. I was lying beside my dog in my dark front yard.

I thought, not for the first time, that the earth, in terms of all the space around it, is a mote of dust, with billions of tiny lives winding out all over it. Sparrows and trout and elephants and apes and ants. Dogs and humans. Life and life and life, life after life, all here on earth together for their flash of time. Viciousness and greed and love and hope and hopelessness, all terminally tangled and intertwined.

The earth and the moon above me seemed worn-out and patient.

My dog settled his head, gently, and fell asleep.

NOTHING?

I guess you know by now—little by little, the
universe created itself. I can't follow the ins and outs,
but, okay, we're on our own. Or God came later,
when we needed something big and calm and
certain because we looked up there at the stars and
caught a glimpse of infinity and so got scared about
our tiny lives blowing through.

But now we know that our infinity is insignificant.
That there are thousands of infinities, piled one on
top of the other, each one of them created, in its
own way, out of nothing. (I can't get that. Nothing?
Where was nothing?) Anyway, each one created
differently, by different accidents, with different
physical laws that turned nothing into different
kinds of something.

And down here on this little beat-up planet, this
cracked nutshell of a world, maybe we've gotten to
another phase, where everything uncreates itself
back into powdery remains, spiraling outward.
Maybe it's happening right now—all these people in
this hotel waking to their busy, consequential lives,
brewing their complimentary coffee in their little
drip pots, stirring in their packets of fake cream,
settling down in their wing chairs, going over their
notes—tiny temporary flickering flares of sensibility
in the accidental universe no one created.

Meanwhile, space blooms overhead, silken waves of energy rise, composed of everything that ever lived and died—even now, our dear departed could be flowing outward past Uranus, creative, potent, on their way to make another world.

THE MOUNTAIN'S TREE

Birds flew from the tree when the tree fell.
Birds circled for hours trying to find their nests
in the empty air. The great root stood up like a house
before the steel blade.

First they pushed the tree into the valley.
Then they pushed the mountain onto the tree
that was on the mountain.

Where did the raccoon and the fox go,
when the mountain began its crashing down,
when the mountain buried the tree?
There were foxes on the mountain
and foxes where the mountain fell.
Where is the path that the boy made
by going to the tree because
it was his favorite tree because
it was the biggest on the mountain,
and sometimes he sat under it, being quiet,
or sometimes he would climb it
because the thick limbs let him.
He could get way up.
He could see everything.

The terrible noise came.
When the steel took the tree
out of the mountain, he heard it
from way down the slope.
He ran and ran. But the steel
had already sent the tree over the edge
and now it was sending the mountain down
on top of the tree and why
and why? Because. And now,
where the tree was
up there in the sky
and he could see it from way far away,
there is no tree.
And where the mountain was
there is no mountain.

IF SPIRIT IS ABROAD THIS DAY

The elm shakes out the light like a sleepy laundress,
reaching with her long arms to pin the sheets.
Every kind of green creeps out of blackness
into the gathering light.

This morning, late in May, some bird is singing
a little song I ought to know the name of.
The woodpecker rattles the day,
drilling oblong slashes in the soffits,
getting at the larvae of the carpenter bees.
Woodpeckers, not bees with their tidy holes,
will bring this house down, I expect, in time—
our dear tin roof. I won't be here to notice.
And Jim is already gone.

If spirit is abroad this day, I want my share of it
to coalesce as gratitude for the ancient elm
beside whose life my own is a dinky thing,
and for tomatoes and cucumbers, volunteering in the garden,
offspring of last year's compost. Let me, too, volunteer.
Let me—after waiting through the long winter
for my chance to germinate when no one asked me to—
come up into the sun to bear unlooked-for fruit.
Let me hear woodpeckers at it early, and—listen!
There's the dove.
Let me not fail to hear whatever calls.

Part Seven: The Known Path, The Way Home

FINAL BLOOD

Their lives pulsing out of their bodies
on a deep night that was meant to celebrate
their joy in the music and in their bodies
moving to the music, but suddenly ripped,
falling, falling out of the music.

This trouble is not for tears anymore.
It is for blood, for final blood,
pulsing out all over everything.
His weapon runs through its first round—
ammo designed not just to kill, but to inflict
maximum bodily harm,
just to be on the safe side.
He reloads, lets loose another thirty fast bullets.
And then again.

Because his life is troublesome.
And so he is murdering his trouble. His trouble,
once all inside of him, is outside now,
in bodies that were loving themselves tonight,
dancing, fondling, flirting, showing their moves,
kissing. These bodies make him sick.
He has multi-rounds, Second Amendment rounds,
NRA freedom to murder the ones who tear his heart out
with their freedom to dance close and sexy.
These bodies make him sick with rage and want.
They kill him. He kills them.

And there they are—the shining faces,
the names, the forty or sixty more years
they might have lived trailing behind them,
ghostly—the ones who were dancing like crazy
just before they fell down dead or dying,
bullets ripping into bodily joy.
I stand before the screen, my own heart
still beating.

DOVE

My slippered foot in the bathroom at five a.m.
nudges against some soft small bulk.
Uh oh. Turn on the light and face it.

In repose, on her side, intact, except for the drifts
of downy feathers covering the white tiled floor—
a gray dove, dead for the sport of it,
brought in and left for me—a gift, I think.
Or an instruction. I get some paper towels
and pick her up, the little weight, the gentle grazer
on the slope of the garden, the mourning caller,
the ancient urgent message: *I'm here! I'm here!*
And the song beneath the song, the solemn *for now*
that every living creature knows,
riding under the throaty, thrilled vibrato.

The killing's done. The cat just wants
to sleep it off at the foot of the bed.

I used to think *passed* was a timid way to not say *died*.
But the dove has passed, I think, through the horror curtain
of fright and pain into the *elsewhere* all around us,
extending outward beyond what we can imagine, so far,
of *far*. I take her half-pound, temporary body
out to the woods and settle her under a tree.

AUTUMNAL

All day the sky has trundled over us,
low-bellied, dense with purpose.
Rumors of rain stir the high, unfallen leaves—
the last gasp of the maples, their high boughs
rising and falling in the sudden wind.
And crows rise up. *Autumnal* is the word
for this heavy sky. The deep thrum, the tumble,
the ommm of autumn. Dark clouds shove upward,
leaving just a crack of brighter gray at the horizon.

I'm a tight little bundle of gratitude, slipping downhill,
here in this outcast, overcast day, this heavy-sky day.
And now a sinking glow, a dim gold tunnel.
The kindly stranger waits there, at its mouth.
I am more joy than you have ever had.
You can't imagine…
                    But, here on this earth,
I've already had almost more joy
than I can stand—lasagna, Trollope, Jim,
and Bach, and sycamore trees, and dogs—
six good dogs, over the years. I don't want
to be taken by the hand and led past
the last outpost of anything familiar
into sweet blackness, blankness.
                    Something
is coming toward me, fast. I turn and run.
The known path. The way home. Now it comes down.
The dogs are running, too. They hear the thunder.

BODY HEAT

A black cat in my lap, purring away,
kneading my belly, cozying up
against my 98.2, and, to some cat-shaped degree,
giving something back.
We're here exchanging body heat,
waiting for the stove to get to work
before we greet the day.

Ah, now I hear the fire taking hold.
I switch on the lamp. He ducks his head
inside the fold of my coat
to hide his eyes from the light.
With a cat on my lap, I manage to write
these lines. But I can't sit here all day—
I have to see to things, get in some wood.
But this is good.

That old black magic pins me to this chair.
I sit here making my cat warm. It's clear
this is my purpose in life.

He purrs and purrs.

HANDS

Look—your hands. In this light
of a summer morning darkening to rain,
they are antiques—generations
of yourself handed them down to you.

Each day, your hands touched, grasped,
ran themselves over things, held things,
stroked, stirred, moved through
lake water, dishwater, bathwater,
through soil as you planted, through air as you spoke,
as you danced, as you hung the clothes on the line.
They moved in their moment and through it to another,
and they are still, though changed,
your hands, in this instant,
in the changing light.

PLAYING
Elegy for Donna Boyd

We were trying to find out again what we had known
as children, that art is play, whatever else it may become.
Music ran under her life like an underground river. She
brought in tambourines and drums and bells for us to fool
around with. We played them together, even though we
didn't know how.

We fell into trances, didn't want to stop. We sounded
wonderful to ourselves.

Later, the last two times before the cancer came for her,
she asked us each to name a note—C sharp, E, B, A flat, say.
Then she went to the piano and gently, attentively played
the notes, listened to them, head bent, body curved
protectively over the keys. Gradually, music would suggest
itself out of the random collection of notes, become more
definite, more formed. It felt as though she were invoking
it, asking it to come up, waiting for it to do so. As we
listened, the melody gathered itself, a structure asserted its
form, beautiful and assured and deep, as it emerged. The
connection between that music and whatever is eternal
was pure, unmistakable, the way it shaped itself, came
together, as if those notes had always been looking for each
other. I heard it. It was gone as soon as it was heard.

She did that for us twice that fall. Then she went on a trip.
When she came back, a month later, we began, all of us
together, Donna's journey toward wherever that music
came from. Wherever it goes back to.

REGINA SUBLIMA IN KENTUCKY
Elegy for Jane Gentry Vance

It has rained all morning. The creeks overflow their
banks. She comes down the stairs in her yellow
sweater, casual, ordinary—her instruction to us of
how we need to be now. She's going to show us how
to do this, now that we know it's ours to do. We've
come, the four of us, for a little party, maybe.

Her house is filled with the bounty of all the lives
on which her own has settled—the treasure of loved
things, the ball of twine her grandma saved, who
never threw away a thing that might someday be
useful, the rugs and crocks and chairs and spoons
passed down to her, collected, used, cherished.
She loves things the years speak out of. They are
a richness to her. Her life is a link.

'Nobody wants this stuff now,' she announces,
cheerfully. 'They'll have a yard sale, I guess.'

I thought you'd make a hundred, Jane. I even knew
the kind of old lady you'd be—lucid and honed and
sure of what pleased you. *Still sharp as a tack*, they'd
say about you in Athens, Kentucky.

'I like those pants,' I blurt out, laughing then at my
absurdity.

She comes right back: 'I'll will them to you.'

Let's do the best we can. A six-to-nine-month party.
Or maybe longer. Let it be longer.

We'll ring ourselves around you. We'll hold you up
now. Love must be good for something.

Meanwhile, Jane, in her yellow sweater, gropes behind
the couch (in May) to unplug the antique electric
Christmas candles, in order to plug in the antique
telephone-booth-sized music box, because we've said
we want to hear it—*Regina Sublima*, it's called, the
name written across its glass front in ornate gold
letters. Her father got it at an auction in 1958.

The huge metal disk begins to spin slowly. And with
resonant sweetness, the melody unwinds—
Weep no more, my lady. Weep no more today.

And so we don't. That's what she's saying. Don't.

NECKLACE OF SHARK'S TEETH
Elegy for Judy Young
After Nafea Faa Ipoipo?, *a painting by Paul Gauguin*

Pilar, in a time before the painting
She was a child, tall for her age, standing at the edge of
the wide sea. Then, suddenly, a wall of water came
toward her. She braced herself. She stood up straight,
waiting for it to break over her.

When it receded, she was still standing. She knew it
was a miracle, because of the necklace of shark's teeth
she found circling her throat. She did not know if this
necklace would protect her or hurt her.

Pilar, in the painting
She has grown up. Her face is calm, but serious, even
wary. Her eyes still know what it means to have
withstood that wave. She is wearing a high-necked
pink dress, as if she were on her way to church. She is
making a sign with her long fingers. I don't know its
meaning. Her story has no words. Her long hair is
caught back at the nape of her neck with flowers. She
still wears the necklace of shark's teeth. She still does
not know whether they will protect her or hurt her,
but she wears them, to remember. So far, they have
protected her, for here she is.

Flo, in the painting
She is the one who moves like water, river water
finding its way along slants of the earth, water moving
sometimes swiftly, sometimes slowly, gathering,
whispering down the rocks.

She is supple—easy and alert. Pilar is restrained, full of
caution, but also alert. Flo finds her way by feeling for
it. She wears sky and water against her skin. She too
has flowers in her hair. Her blouse drapes low, her feet
are bare. She is about to rise, to move.

Flo and Pilar, there together in the grass, not quite
touching, but close. Though they are not alike, they are
easy together. Gauguin thinks they are asking each other
when they will marry. But they are not. Pilar, making her
mysterious long-fingered sign, knows what she knows,
keeping it a secret, inside her. Flo is all in her body.
Behind them, two faraway figures are coming across a
long field, one in a rosy color and one in shadowy blue.
Flo and Pilar do not see them yet.

THERE
Elegy for Audrey Robinson

The earth orbits round the sun reliably,
doing its dainty balletic spins as it goes.
From a galactic distance, you'd think you were seeing
a serene, well-mannered little planet,
but when you get right down to it,
the motion of this world is a tumbling motion—
we tumble from light to dark, then back again,
through long, bleached summer days and velvet nights,
through barking nights of frost,
and early winter dark falling like years, too soon…

Oh, I don't want to write your blinking elegy.
I want to call you up and have another
of our existential hour-long conversations
about *there*. You were a student of *there*. You were
my transcendental link.
The trouble is, I can't believe you're gone—
See? I can't even say that other word.
Gone where? The wind rushes into the void.
I don't know where you went. I just know
you've left a hole in the world where once there was
your joyful, willful, grumpy warrior mode,
your fiercely living, pliant, surprising self,
the wild woman who explained
the foibles of the world through cartoon strips
of a little figure, often found sitting in lotus pose

in a little transparent box,
then lured one way or another
into the tricky world.
                              I want you to be
like a firefly some child has caught in a jar—
so as to watch its lights for a while—and then
(reluctantly) releases. Freed, the firefly loops upward,
flashing wildly to signal to the rest, *I am here! Here I still am!*

Where are you, Audrey? Where is *there*?
I look for you, slicing through air
with your intricate, clean, decisive karate moves.
Send us a message, flash your life in the fallen leaves.

Say: *Here I still am.* Say: *There* is *here.*

METAPHORS FOR THE SOUL
Elegy for Carolyn Hisel

(Please help me) paint the transcendent metaphor.
                    Prayer, from the journal of C.H.

Soul was what you were asking to see—
and asking us to see with you.
That's what those paintings were always about,
isn't it, the ones where the almost-breathing light
shone through veil after mysterious veil,
with some attentive, fragile figure near the back,
touched by it, receiving it,
standing stilled and stunned by it,
changed by it, becoming part of it.

Or not—those lumpy, awkward, comical little guys—
were they not also soul? Yapping and yelling,
here in the sharp-edged world, jolly, mad,
frightened, forlorn, with their shopping bags
and tricycles and roller coasters
and helicopter caps and violins.

And then the landscapes—
peaceful rowboats drifting on calm lakes,
or water running between strict banks
out to the wild sea. Towers—mysteriously precise,
as though erected for a function
we weren't meant to understand,
or way out there in the distance, rising up,

154

half-hidden in fog. The steps down into deep woods,
full of strange flowers and misshapen trees.
The mysterious houses, made of light,
and the earthbound, familiar houses
with their sofas and pianos and kitchen tables,
and—always—windows, looking out,
light falling through the half-drawn curtains
and people waiting for something, with caution
or glee or terror or calm familiarity.

I get it now, Carolyn—those images
you dove into infinity to find.
It was always soul you were after, wasn't it.
Even the menacing brutes, the wild dancers,
the thin-armed, lost girls, the comfortable grannies
in their aprons—they were all metaphors
for the soul.

I want to tell you—can you hear me, there,
where you so suddenly are,
in the tower across the river?—that I see now,
not heaven, but this very world,
everywhere opening into soul.

LAKE OF DAY

slowly the darkness opens slowly it is a gray lake
holding me holding me
I remember something I remember my name
it slides into the deep underneath me
the wide all around me

new air moves cool secret over my skin
my eyes are open color comes in now
green clasps me green pulls me forward
lifts me in its tall arms

then a sharp shadow falls on the wall
light all around it
from the shore voices call
wake up

indigo yellow crimson
enter in

all day
I am remembering
that gray lake
that floating

NO LANGUAGE

I pull up silence like a comforter.
I lie beneath it, thinking
of nothing. Sometimes
this is not difficult
at all, my life till now
coiled neatly in the corner,
detached from me. I'm happy here,
almost. My mind gone, silence
blouses out and seems
like truth. No image here,
no language, no remembering.
Only the old cicadas
of the inner ear, the marred
but steady silence.
Nothing else. Hold on.

But his hands were beautiful
that now are ash.

IF YOU CAME BACK NOW

you would find me
you would find me where
you left me
you will not come back
you are gone I can't find you
you are nowhere you were once

once you were everywhere I turned
you were coming up the stone path
one slim hand beating time
to whatever the invisible words were
the other holding an empty cup
I am holding an empty cup

no one is coming
up the stone path
dearest dearest
I can hardly move
but you're the one
who's dead

AFTER THE LAST FROST DATE

Days slide by like water now,
liquid, flowing down to the sea.
We're carried on the current,
glinting in the light as we go by.

Here is March, the green world
waiting to come forth, coming forth,
the lilac buds swelling, spikes of bulbs
poking up through dead grass,
as always, as always,
with great force and certainty.

Clumps of daffodils rise now
in the field by the creek, where,
a hundred and fifty years ago, maybe,
some woman planted them near her cabin
with sweet, domestic hope.
The cabin is long-gone. But the bulbs
may come back forever.
They are what's left.

Eternal life right there, maybe.

EVER AFTER

I think of where I am now as *inside.*
Outside is where *we* were, where change was,
where things moved and shuddered,
screamed and laughed and turned out right
or wrong. Inside, the air is thin.
I call it ether. It moves in a thin way.
This may be ever after. It's nice with dogs,
with long light as the sun goes down
and maybe this is what I always wanted.
I don't know. Not wanting anything
is what I want right now.
                    Only,
when I'm asleep, the old desires break through
and come inside. I dreamt last night
I was flying. I did cartwheels and twirls
up there, in a beaded coat. It was hard work,
but I remained aloft. I love to sleep and wake.
I wake inside the ring of nothing doing,
turn on the light, and burrow into the pillows
with my mystery.

Part Eight: The Rain Goes On Without You

BRIGHTNESS

All this Italian tumbling out—throaty robust alto,
ecstatic soprano, a soaring duet. No, now it's a regular
choral event, seven unconstrained Italians under the
stone arch, all talking—well, shouting, really—at once.
The extravagant, ordinary world of other people.

I wish I could understand what's so funny.

I'm in the trellised garden, a little removed. A soft
breeze from the hills drifts in around me. Here's an
Italian ant, crawling up my arm. And now, abrupt
silence. Great, sharp ridges of ancient silence. Where
did they go? The Italians?

The arch they were standing under a minute ago is
at least a thousand years old.

Precise dark shadows of small clouds skim like skiffs
over the fielded floor of the valley down there. People
lived here, farmed here, made wine, baked bread, stored
grain and hay, yelled greetings and curses, slaughtered
wild boars and lambs and cattle, had groves of figs and
olives, had graves, had children. Fought to own these
hills, wave after wave of them. And here the place still is.

Where I come from, we don't have much history to
speak of. We have history not to speak of—what we

used to call pre-history. Pre-contact now, a nicer way of
saying that whatever happened before we landed is
really over. No-trace history, erased history, Industrial-
versus-Stone-Age history—a few bones and ash pits and
caves and shards of pottery, the big blasted *before* of
things, to keep the archaeologists among us busy. We're
curious, now. But that past is not *our* past. The long-
gone past of almost all of us happened somewhere else.

Here, in this place, time reaches backwards. That land
down there was marshland. People came and drained it
and made fields, built walled cities on hilltops, made
cunning ornaments and tools, chiseled rooms and
corridors out of the volcanic stone beneath their houses,
where they pressed grapes and olives and, in war, hid
from and ambushed the next lot who tried to take their
town. The Romans and Christ came later.

That's the short course in Italian history.

Now we visitors from the New World stumble into
duomos, their spires yearning heavenward. We ponder
the bones of saints, the splinters of the cross in the
golden reliquary, St. Francis' very tunic (he was so
small)—the intricate, illuminated layers of meaning in
the forever-unfolding story of why we're here and what
we have to do to triumph over death. Frescoes,

resurrected from centuries of whitewash and old plaster, appear and disappear—glowing pastel ghosts. The colors, once bold and primary and certain, have attained a quality of tender speculation—almost, sometimes, of pure transparency, more vision than history.

A hesitant, dumbfounded girl receives the Annunciation she cannot refuse. Or, eyes cast down in worried love, she touches her long fingers to the chin of the elderly infant in her lap, as if to assure herself that he is real, or perhaps to comfort him for what she begins to feel is coming toward them. In back of her, the sweet, ordered gardens of Tuscany unfold—arbors and groves, a homey, familiar landscape, nothing uncontrollable or wild. But immensities of trouble and tragedy loom—not only the Crucifixion. Arrows, knives, beheadings, stacks of tinder at the martyrs' feet, dogs with their teeth in men's arms, all faithfully recounted on the walls of the storied, story-filled cathedral. And then, the crucifixes everywhere, so insistently imagined—the horrid nails driven into the flesh, the dripping blood, the body of Christ, stretched and suffering and almost naked— creations powered by desperate faith, and also, to my jaded twenty-first century eyes, by something like erotic fascination with undefended pain.

But I'm from somewhere else.

White cabbage moths, the same as we have back home,
I think, flutter in. A tree frog suddenly blasts again and
again an urgent, electronic cry. It sounds like a warning.

I don't believe in anything but this breeze—

Oh, and those children last night in Castiglione del
Lago, those wide-awake children playing Statues at
eleven p.m., in the cobbled street, freezing in High
Renaissance attitudes, small bodies torqued in writhing
tragedy or arms-flung-upward joy. The children of the
children of the children who came into this brightness
and disappeared.

Yesterday, at the crown of a high stone hill, in a walled
town built of that stone eight hundred years before the
birth of Christ, crowds poured out of the *duomo* (built
more recently, in the 1200s) after Sunday evening Mass.
Everyone in town—in flowered hats, in jeans, in tights
and T-shirts, in suits and uniforms, in coveralls and
aprons—had been inside. I watched from the steps.

When the nave had finally emptied, I crept in to look at
the frescoes in the last light.

MANHATTAN'S GHOST

A rising-up, out of the wide sidewalk, sharp-edged, particular. A glimpse, a flash, gone fast—a forest, a steep outcropping of rock, a river.

Then I was back again with the taxis, the waxing parlors, the taquerias. Broadway, the high Eighties.

I put it down to city adrenalin, sleeplessness.

I didn't live here anymore.

It happened again. I almost hate to say it. Three more times. On St. Mark's Place, on Fifth near Central Park, up near Columbia. I'd lived in each of these neighborhoods, but it wasn't my own life here that I was seeing. My life, its moment in this place, the stupendous place itself—I don't know— sank down into the concrete and asphalt. What rose up—no, there was no rising, it was just calmly *there*, an immense contained silence and watchfulness. An alert waiting.

These visions, glimpses—what should I call them, hallucinations?—were fast, but vivid. Rocky bluffs, a wide river running along down there between them. Trees, their trunks glinting in the sun along the banks of the river. At first, I didn't see the boats.

I only saw the river, the trees, a few silent people,
waiting along the bank—curious, interested,
not fearful, it seemed.

But then the boats did come. The boats landed.
Men disembarked. They brought their tools with
them. The silent people watched and then—

The streets lined with stores, the mounds of oranges
and artichokes, the dresses in hopeful, brash colors
for the spring that will come again, we believe.
The massive buildings, full of money and plans.
The music, the hustle and funk, the flat-out
desperation and desire. The steam vents smelling
of laundry soap and garlic. The wooden walkways
around construction sites. The people hunched in
their March layers against the wind, waiting for the
light to change. The guy selling knock-off watches.
The orchestra tuning up for Mahler.

Later, leaving the city, I saw from the air the vast
construction, the sheer weight, the piles of glass
and girders, catching the sun.

The little island, its two rivers. The sea beyond.

SUBLET

Out of the subway at one a.m., along the cross street
with the shop called *Religious Sex*—leather jockstraps,
crotchless underpants, whips, chains, collars, stunned
and humble under the stern fluorescent glare.
Four blocks east past the baths, the all-night tempura bar.
Some drunk leans in murmuring, 'I like 69.'
I find the edges of the square key in my pocket,
hold onto it, cut side up.

The door swings shut, locks again behind me.
The grimy vestibule of my heart.
The jimmied mailboxes of my heart.
Two flights, two flights,
the round key, the round table, the smell of gas,
the gray cloth covering the window
that stares straight into someone else's life,
two feet away—a room lit from another room,
beyond. The clanking radiator of my heart.
I lose myself in a dream of rooms,
one opening on the next,
none known to me.

At dawn, in Tompkins Square,
a man in a leather jacket perches
on the back of a bench, feet on the seat.
A woman stands before him, her long gray coat
blowing around her. They're laughing,

flapping their arms. She is a pigeon,
he a hawk, rising now, as if lifting off,
to stand on the seat, his back arching slowly,
his throat in the end arched too and exposed
as his flapping arms attain the zenith
reverse their motion with eloquent wrists,
and he settles again to the back of the bench.
The woman, meanwhile, continues to laugh
and flap and yell, *Fly! Fly!*
But he's tired of the game.
                                        And I run on,
out of the park, under a ghost caught in a tree,
past the last of a garden where a building is gone,
but another is coming, soon enough.
I turn back, heart pumping, pull up at the corner
of A and Eighth, buy a croissant and the *Times*.

At the round table in front of the window,
I watch two corgis down in the garden
digging a serious hole at the fence.
On the other side of the kitchen wall,
the scales begin. Then Mozart all morning.
I'm practicing, too, lost in this work,
muttering, counting.

When the flautist stops for lunch,
I put on the song I've been loving all week,
the imperfect, passionate voice, the blind tenor,
Time to say goodbye. I boil water for tea,
scramble some eggs.
                              My life holds.
The long scar holds over my heart.
The flautist begins the scales again,
sailing up to the zenith, finding the way,
over and over, then falling back,
like a scrap in the wind,
to come to rest.

THROUGH

Through the dark, deep-rooted elms behind me
in this still morning before light comes,
through birds that love the berries of the mistletoe,
then drop its seeds among the branches,
causing a merry winter riot, festoons of green
that may bring these old trees down one day,
through the ladybugs clustered in a ball
deep in the woodpile for the winter—
through light years of emptiness
cupping this scrim of local morning fog,

through the brother cats someone dumped on the road
ten years ago when they were tiny kittens,
who made their way somehow, wild and starving,
past coyotes and owls to our back door,
so scared they lived for two months under the glider,
two or three more before they let us touch them—
now curled together at the foot of the bed,

through every living thing that trails its own small story
something moves, transparent, something like breath,
only continuous, not in and out, just *through*,
not needing any apparatus except its one intention.
                          More like wind
                          or downhill flowing water.

Now, through the girl in the off-white coat waiting with me
for the light to change at the corner of Lime and Main,
through each person decked out in Wildcat-blue
headed toward the game, through the people
coming out of church, through the brunch-eaters,
the late sleepers under quilts, or on top of heating grates
on the street this frigid day—

Let this moving thing like wind not be caught, or caught only
in something like tall white sails rigged to a sturdy mast,
something made to move in pure response.

Let it never be waylaid, locked up
in some tight-cornered airlessness
where it thickens and clots—
in the mind, for instance, of some crazed young man.
Let it not be caught and taught there how to live
forever, and exactly how forever will unfold,
and how to use that young man's body as righteous fuse,
so that the ones who do not agree, exactly,
might be blown up in the marketplace.

And let it not be halted, either,
by my own encumbered self,
by my sloth and vanity and fear.

173

Let it flow through me unhampered.
Let its gift be its motion.
Let me know it as a gift.
Or not know it. Let it go on
without my notice.
Let me never impede it in its course
through this vast blowing world.
And some day or night to come,
let me join its swift gliding,
leaving behind only what it passed through.

THE BRIGHT FEAR

The early sun shot under the morning clouds
at a low slant, so that each thing it struck,
each rock and stalk of weed,
seemed more itself than it had ever been.
I didn't know it was raining until I saw,
in the small creek that crosses the path through the bottom,
tiny circles playing the surface. Even when
I held my hand out, turned my face to the sky,
I couldn't feel the rain hitting my skin,
so warm and fine it was. The path curved round—
I walked directly toward the sun. And then
the air was full of streaks of brightness,
slanting rain catching the slanting light
as if the light poured down onto our earth
through pinholes in the sky. *The light of heaven*
come down to us, I thought, *as secret rain.*

But then the old fear entered: *you will lose this world,*
You know you will. It is pierced by death
coming down on rocks and grass. It falls on you,
whether you feel it or not.

Still, I walked forward through shafts of radiance
made from the bright, small drops.

MATISSE: *LA FENÊTRE OUVERTE*
The Phillips Collection, Washington, DC

Last week, at the Phillips Collection,
I walked past moments of light
caught in gold frames. Voices cried out
from the canvases: *Look! Look!*
This is what I saw when I was here.
The peaches, the boats, the bay.
The rooftops, wheat fields, tables.
Faces in light. Light. Colors, fast, passing.
Colors struggling, rough and thick, toward form.
Dense colors standing still, like gravestones,
but also passing.

                    Beside each painting,
the necessary placard—parentheses
to frame the span of the painter's life, two hands
cupping the years like thistledown,
to keep them from flying away.

An open window, casement thrown wide, a cliff
beyond. And then the sea and sky. Light streaming
through the orange-gold room. The woman,
half-awake in the light blue chair, the black cat…

This is what I was when I was here. [1869–1947]
Who knows what those dates held? The days are gone.
What's left—stilled instants, scooped from the stream of life.
I saw them there, at the Phillips.

Home from that journey,
I sit on the edge of the deck, looking up.
I've been waiting a long time for things to get this still.
The tender light of high October rests along the ridge tops.
The old elms reach out to touch it. As I do here,
with these lines.

The clear yellow light.
The bright still air.

THE RUNNING

The big print Jim made of one of his photographs,
the one that hangs over the bed, fell during the night—
the horse running, its form distilled
to the essence of its motion,
like the form in a cave painting.
One of his last. Its falling did not wake me.
It could have landed on my head.
Instead, it slid straight down the wall
and lodged behind the mattress.

If I have lost everything
that came before this moment,
what is there to lose?

This! This! the running horse says.
The running! It's the running,
not the horse—

THE RAIN GOES ON WITHOUT YOU

It's raining at last. Relief steams on the red tin roof.
The roof shines in the sudden afternoon darkness.
Lightning throbs far off under the horizon,
a fluttering pulse. You stand at the door.
You know how to move, not just to stand still,
and so you walk through the door
into the rain after the wind has stilled,
into the thick cedar woods, the longest day,
another half-year gone.

The cedars release their spirits to the drenching air.
Their boughs hang down in heavy wetness.
The rain falls softly all around you. Your soul
may be like the resinous scent
that lifts from the dripping noiseless cedars.

Lie down now on the soft bed of fallen needles.
Hush. Your life is a minor event in the chain of solstices,
in the eternal coming and going, a little coalescence.
Pretend you are asleep.
Pretend you are not anymore.
The rain goes on without you,
the small lightnings come and go
above where you are not.

THE GREAT OAK ON THE RIDGE

High up, the ornate ceremony of disappearance
is nearly complete, a small, final glow
not yet let go of, lifted toward the sky.
But it's the stalwart form of the tree's revealed shape
that takes the stark, long-shadow-casting light
this afternoon, my own thin shadow
stilled on a ridge of rock beside it.
Here, for this instant, has no name.

Then earth breaks through,
the chorus of many things —
the tall blowing winter weeds,
the long clouds moving sideways
across the west, one crow,
headed homeward, and myself,
in my old tan jacket and scuffed-up boots,
turning and going on.

Acknowledgments

I WOULD LIKE TO THANK Gray Zeitz, editor of Larkspur Press, and Bob Baris, editor of the Press on Scroll Road, for permission to publish poems that first appeared in their handset letterpress limited editions. I have included Scroll Road's *Joy Dogs* in its entirety in Part Five, adding a few more recent poems to that section. Twenty-one poems from Larkspur's *Dividing Ridge* are scattered throughout the text. It has been a great and ongoing pleasure to me to see my poetry presented with such care and artistry in the books they have produced.

And I am more grateful than I can say to Nyoka Hawkins, editor and publisher of Old Cove Press, for her expertise (literary, graphic, and digital), her generosity of spirit, and dynamic energy in getting my poetry gathered and presented herein. Without her help, patience, and vision, I'm afraid absolutely nothing would have been accomplished.

The following friends have read for me and given me significant help and encouragement: Helen Bartlett, George Ella Lyon, Anne Marie Macari, and Cia White. Most particularly, Susan Starr Richards and Cecilia Woloch both came at it early and often. And I must acknowledge my sisters in this life of art, in whose nurturing company (we met every three weeks for twenty years or so) many of these poems were conceived. Five of the seven of us have recently died. I list their names here, in sadness and continuing disbelief, but also in pride, to have had such friends: Donna Boyd,

Jane Vance, Judy Young, Audrey Robinson, and, as this book was going to press, Carolyn Hisel. Susan Richards and I survive. Sue has been my indispensable friend and writing companion since we were juniors in high school. She and her husband, Dick Richards, are responsible for my ending up in Kentucky forty years ago. Their beautiful farm, in the midst of which I live, is one of the chief pleasures of my life. The privilege of living here has been further enhanced by having Anna and Paul Isaacs and Barb and Dave Lawler as neighbors and the best kind of friends.

I also wish to thank my family, just for being my dear family, beginning with my brothers, Edmund Haynes Taylor and Philip Arnett Taylor, and my stepsons, Lawrence Russell Pemble, Matthew Russell Hall, and Michael Walker Hall. And my sisters- and daughters-in-law: Jan Ziegel Taylor and Darlene Spurlock Taylor, Melissa Booth Hall and Lisa Costiloe Hall. And the amazing offspring of them all, now beginning to roll on, once or twice, into a fourth generation. And my friends from so far back they seem like sisters, Joanne Race Frederick and Anne Barbara Bard. And Paula Dunaway Merwin, whose absence from the world she inhabited so fully, and from my life, is still impossible for me to comprehend.

Lastly, I want to acknowledge the continuing gift to me from my late husband, James Baker Hall. His questing spirit and devotion to his art—his absolute passion for it—and his belief in me have been a light through the tunnel of my own doubt and hesitation. Also, he left me a band of young

184

people, moving on now into middle-age, whom I treasure but dare not name for fear of leaving someone out. You all know who you are. I believe Jim thanks you, too. He and I have to give special gratitude to Sarah Wylie Ammerman VanMeter, his archivist, whose common sense and grace have over and over saved the day and brought simple light to complicated matters.

—M. A. Taylor-Hall

About the Author

MARY ANN TAYLOR-HALL began writing poetry at the age of ten. Her father sent one of her poems (which began 'Our childhood days are over! Soon it will be our time...') to *The Saturday Evening Post*, which rejected it with a gentle note. She began writing fiction at the University of Florida, where she studied under Andrew Lytle, and has considered herself a fiction writer for most of her writing life.

She has published two novels: *Come and Go, Molly Snow* and *At The Breakers*, and a collection of stories, *How She Knows What She Knows About Yo-Yos*. Her short fiction has been published in *The Paris Review*, *The Kenyon Review*, *Ploughshares*, *Shenandoah*, *The Sewanee Review*, and other literary quarterlies, and has been anthologized in *Best American Short Stories*. In the past ten years, she has returned to poetry and has published two previous collections, *Dividing Ridge* and *Joy Dogs*. She has been the recipient of two grants from the National Endowment for the Arts and a grant from the Kentucky Arts Council.

Born in Chicago, Taylor-Hall moved with her family to Central Florida when she was seven. After receiving her M.A. degree from Columbia University, she spent two migratory decades before settling on a farm in Harrison County, Kentucky, with, until his death several years ago, her husband, the poet James Baker Hall. She still lives there, with two old dogs and three cats.